ASIA BEYOND GROWTH

Urbanization in the World's Fastest-changing Continent

ORO *editions*
Publishers of Architecture, Art, and Design
Gordon Goff – Publisher
USA: PO Box 998, Pt Reyes Station, CA 94956
Asia: Block 8, Lorong Bakar Batu #02-04, Singapore 348743
www.oroeditions.com
info@oroeditions.com

Copyright © 2010 by ORO *editions*

ISBN: 978-0-9795395-1-0

AΞCOM

Edited by EDAW, now the Design + Planning Practice at AECOM.
AECOM's Design + Planning practice brings together landscape architects, urban designers and planners,
ecologists, environmental planners and economic planners. We make distinctive and successful places.
We embrace complexity at all scales, within all contexts, worldwide. We are part of AECOM, a versatile
and collaborative community of designers and engineers. Learn more at www.aecom.com.

Graphic Design: ORO *studio* and theBookDesigners
Production: Gordon Goff, Joanne Tan and Davina Tjandra
Color Separation and Printing: ORO *group* Ltd

AECOM and ORO *editions* have made every effort to minimize the overall carbon footprint of this project.
As part of this goal, we, in association with Global ReLeaf, have arranged to plant two trees for each and every
tree used in the manufacturing of the paper produced for this book. Global ReLeaf is an international campaign
run by American Forests, the nation's oldest nonprofit conservation organization. Global ReLeaf is American
Forests' education and action program that helps individuals, organizations, agencies, and corporations improve
the local and global environment by planting and caring for trees.

Throughout this book, various pieces of data are cited, or were calculated based on existing data from reputable
public sources. Neither AECOM nor ORO *editions* take any responsibility for the accuracy of statistics cited in this
publication. Their use is intended as reference only.

North American and International Distribution:
Publishers Group West
1700 Fourth Street
Berkeley, CA 94710
USA
www.pgw.com

CONTENTS

In Asia, growth is the shape of our time. Economies may ebb and flow, but at the heart, the arc of the world from Shanghai to Mumbai to Dubai and locales in between, is a zone of upward transformation. In recent years and decades, we have seen here populations exploding, investments soaring, cities bursting onto the scene, societies progressing, buildings springing up, wealth fomenting and ecosystems failing. It is a familiar story: hyper-growth throws societies, systems and structures into upheaval, and existing built, natural and social environments struggle to adjust. Growth goes from good to bad. This is why we must…

...beyond...

FOREWORD

This is a visual story about placemaking in transition.

Initiated by the land planning and design firm, EDAW, which is now AECOM's Design + Planning practice, the following pages are witness to the remarkable transformation that has taken place on the Asian continent. Through powerful photography, exploration of a handful of innovative projects (both ours and from others), and an atlas of intriguing data, we attempt to tell a story about what happens to cities that are in the midst of massive change.

Our presence in Asia began in 1997, with a two-person office in Hong Kong. Like the economies of Asia, we grew there too; today, we have 400 professionals across 6 studios across the region. And since 2005, we have been part of AECOM. Formed from some of the world's leading consultancies, AECOM works at all contexts and at all scales, integrating Design + Planning, Architecture, Economics, Building Engineering, Program + Construction Management, and technical expertise in Environment, Water, Transportation, Energy and Government Services. Our interdisciplinary work brings together the design of public realm, the master planning of new communities, the restoration of damaged ecosystems, and the regeneration of major urban cores. In this process, we have participated in a great deal of progress, for both public and private clients. We have created meaningful places, rooted in local qualities. But what informs that work? What have we seen in the process?

Over the past decade, as individual practitioners, we have lived in the world's largest continent and witnessed it rapidly become the engine of global economic development – even as the global economy has softened in the past year. We have seen a region on the crest of cultural and commercial transformations that will be especially urban in nature as it is home to 17 of the world's 25 largest metropolitan areas. As millions of people continue to move from countryside to city – as they have in China and are doing in places such as India – there are acute pressures on environmental stewardship and cultural heritage, which are exacerbated by the desires of affluence.

This is why the scale, scope and multifaceted nature of Asia calls for a land-based perspective that is not only comprehensive – bringing together the creative and the technical – but also rooted in a deep philosophy that is contextually sensitive and appreciative of the places in which the work is done.

This is what *Asia Beyond Growth* is about – an exercise in forging that philosophy. Our work is informed by an approach that looks beyond growth. Behind the numbers of impressive economic output and aggressive public investment, we see the connections between wealth and education, infrastructure and ecology, global and local. To the outsider, the frenetic pace and nature of a developing city may seem overwhelming. For the city planner, the landscape architect or the architect, or the ecologist, they should be exciting because they offer so much opportunity to do things right.

We refer to the term 'Emerging World' often in the following pages. Our understanding is that this refers to the geographic arc from Shanghai to Mumbai to Dubai. Its primary engine is China, and it includes Southeast Asia, the Indian subcontinent and the emirates in the Middle East. What all these places share in common are rapidity, density and a lack of complacency. Neighbors, they are fast-paced, heavily populated and ambitious. They are urban. Most interestingly, these places are intensely visual and full of color, which this book attempts to capture through rich imagery of a continent's emerging cityscape.

A VISUAL ATLAS OF A CONTINENT'S EMERGING CITYSCAPE.

AN

RBAN MOMENT

HERITAGE: In Taiyuan, China, traditional architectural forms that have endured for thousands of years are overwhelmed by the new.

WEALTH: In Dubai, gold jewelry on sale speaks to a rapid increase in fortunes. Since 2000, the economies of the UAE, China and India have all more than doubled in size.

NEW EXPERIENCES: In Bangkok, foreign tourists find their way, just as tens of millions of others who are now coming to Asia.

NEW PLACES: In Dubai, largely new residents speed by in new cars on new highways intersecting new buildings.

LEISURE: In Manila, a lone golfer enjoys a game. Tourism development is transforming Asian landscapes, creating intriguing juxtapositions.

ENVIRONMENT: In Bangkok (left) and Beijing (right), automobile traffic grinds to a halt. Currently in Beijing, one in twelve has access to a car. What will happen when one in two do?

NEW CITIES: In Shanghai, young crowds enjoy a sunset along the Huangpu River with the skyscrapers of Pudong as a backdrop. Pudong, which barely existed 15 years ago, today contains two of the world's tallest buildings and has become the visual calling card for the city.

NEWER CITIES: In Dubai, construction cranes light the night building a new Pudong. Most prominent is the Burj Dubai (to the left), which will be the world's tallest building, with 160 floors over more than 800 meters.

PEOPLE: In Mumbai, thousands of people on their daily commute. Four billion people live in Asia, or roughly 60% of the world's total population.

MOVING FORWARD: In Bangkok, a tuk-tuk driver navigates increasingly boisterous streets.

BIG

ER FOOTPRINTS

TODAY FOR THE FIRST TIME IN HISTO
WORLD'S POPULATION LIVES IN CITIE
IN ASIA.

THERE ARE

194

CITIES WITH MORE THAN ONE

AND

56
IN THE AMERICAS, **43** IN EUROPE, **37** IN AFRICA, A

MORE THAN HALF OF THE
AND MOST OF THOSE CITIES ARE

PEOPLE ON THE CONTINENT OF ASIA.

OCEANIA.

EMERGING WORLD CITIES WITH POPU

SEOUL	23,400,000	XI'AN	4,657,000
MUMBAI	21,600,000	PUNE	4,625,000
DELHI	21,500,000	SINGAPORE	4,600,000
SHANGHAI	17,500,000	NANJING	4,575,000
CALCUTTA	15,700,000	KUALA LUMPUR	4,525,000
MANILA	15,600,000	CHITTAGONG	4,350,000
JAKARTA	15,100,000	HARBIN	4,250,000
KARACHI	15,100,000	HANGZHOU	3,925,000
GUANGZHOU	14,700,000	SHANTOU	3,925,000
BEIJING	12,800,000	PYONGYANG	3,675,000
DHAKA	12,600,000	BUSAN	3,575,000
TEHRAN	12,100,000	KANPUR	3,475,000
SHENZHEN	9,150,000	DALIAN	3,375,000
BANGKOK	8,650,000	JINAN	3,275,000
WUHAN	8,650,000	QINGDAO	3,200,000
TIANJIN	8,000,000	BANDUNG	3,175,000
LAHORE	7,950,000	FUZHOU	3,125,000
CHENNAI	7,850,000	JIDDAH	3,125,000
BANGALORE	7,350,000	FAISALABAD	3,100,000
HYDERABAD	7,150,000	TAIYUAN	3,100,000
HONG KONG	7,100,000	KUNMING	3,075,000
TAIPEI	6,700,000	JAIPUR	3,050,000
BAGHDAD	6,250,000	ZHENGZHOU	3,025,000
CHONGQING	6,200,000	RAWALPINDI	2,975,000
AHMEDABAD	5,650,000	SURABAYA	2,950,000
DONGGUAN	5,500,000	AMMAN	2,850,000
CHENGDU	5,450,000	LUCKNOW	2,800,000
HO CHI MINH	5,450,000	KAOHSIUNG	2,775,000
SHENYANG	5,050,000	KABUL	2,750,000
RIYADH	4,775,000	NAGPUR	2,700,000
YANGOON	4,700,000	DAEGU	2,675,000

ONS IN EXCESS OF 1 MILLION

MEDAN	2,650,000	VADODARA	1,870,000
CHANGSHA	2,575,000	DAMMAM	1,860,000
MESHED	2,550,000	JILIN	1,830,000
COLOMBO	2,450,000	COIMBATORE	1,820,000
SUZHOU	2,450,000	BAOTOU	1,810,000
PATNA	2,350,000	BHOPAL	1,810,000
TASHKENT	2,350,000	MULTAN	1,740,000
SHIJIAZHUANG	2,325,000	KUWAIT CITY	1,730,000
GUIYANG	2,275,000	CEBU	1,730,000
URUMQI	2,275,000	LUDHIANA	1,730,000
ZIBO	2,275,000	PALEMBANG	1,730,000
LANZHOU	2,250,000	CHANGZHOU	1,720,000
TAICHUNG	2,225,000	AGRA	1,700,000
ANSHAN	2,200,000	KOCHI	1,660,000
HANOI	2,175,000	SEMARANG	1,660,000
QUANZHOU	2,175,000	VISHAKHAPATNAM	1,610,000
NANCHANG	2,125,000	MEERUT	1,600,000
NINGBO	2,050,000	XUZHOU	1,590,000
BHILAI-RAIPUR	2,025,000	ASANSOL	1,580,000
NANNING	2,025,000	BHUBANESWAR	1,560,000
ISFAHAN	1,960,000	TAEJON	1,550,000
XIAMEN	1,960,000	CHANDIGARH	1,520,000
SANA'A	1,950,000	DUBAI	1,520,000
ZHONGSHAN	1,930,000	GAZA	1,520,000
TANGSHAN	1,920,000	YANTAI	1,520,000
TAOYUAN	1,920,000	GWANGJU	1,500,000
WENZHOU	1,910,000	PESHAWAR	1,500,000
GUJRANWALA	1,900,000	QIQIHAR	1,500,000
BAKU	1,890,000	LUOYANG	1,490,000
HEFEI	1,870,000	MECCA	1,490,000
INDORE	1,870,000	VARANASI	1,470,000

43 in Europe

12 in North America

37 in Africa

44 in Latin America

MILLION-PLUS
MUNICIPALITIES

☐ 10 million +

☐ 5-10 million

☐ 1-5 million

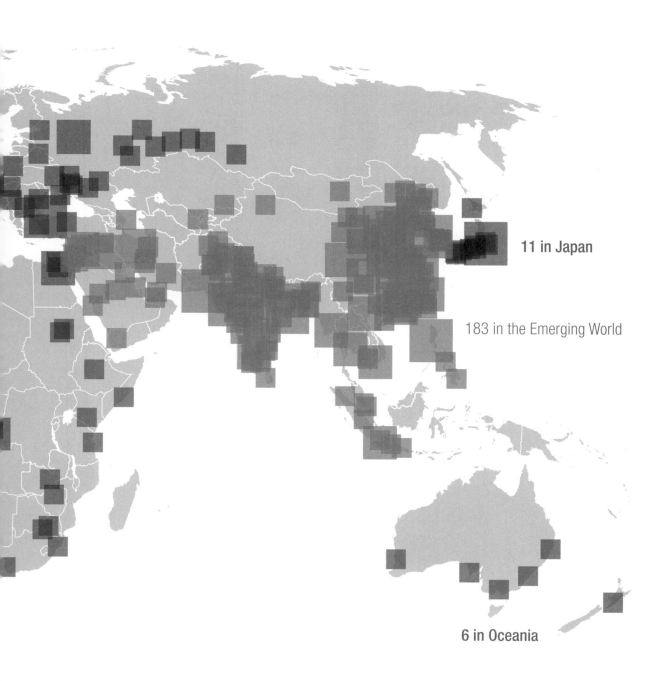

11 in Japan

183 in the Emerging World

6 in Oceania

ASIA'S CITIES ARE INCREASINGLY MEGA.

OF THE WORLD'S TEN LARGEST METROPOLITAN AREAS, 7 ARE ASIAN.

ASIA

OF THE URBAN AGGLOMERATIONS WITH MORE THAN 10 MILLION PEOPLE, HALF ARE ASIAN.

IN JUST 2 COUNTRIES ALONE – **CHINA AND INDIA** THERE ARE MORE THAN **130 MILLION-PLUS CITIES.**

INDIA

CHINA

MEGA CITIES

METROPOLITAN AREAS WITH
MORE THAN 10 MILLION RESIDENTS

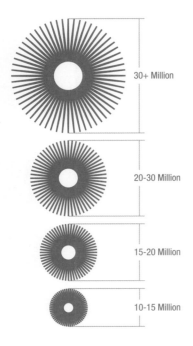

30+ Million

20-30 Million

15-20 Million

10-15 Million

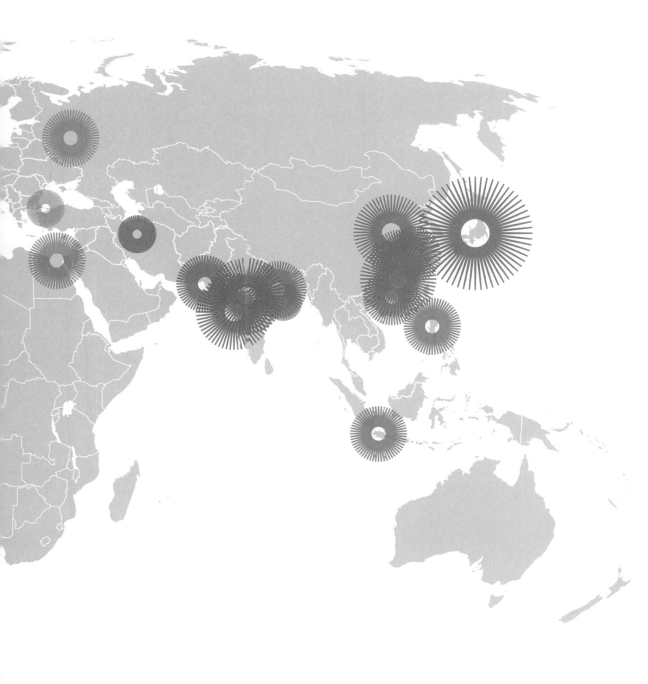

WORLD'S 20 FASTEST GROWING CITIES

TOLUCA

SANTA CRUZ

BAMAKO

LAGOS

LUANDA

KINSHASA

LUBUMBASHI

ASIAN

AFRICAN + LATIN

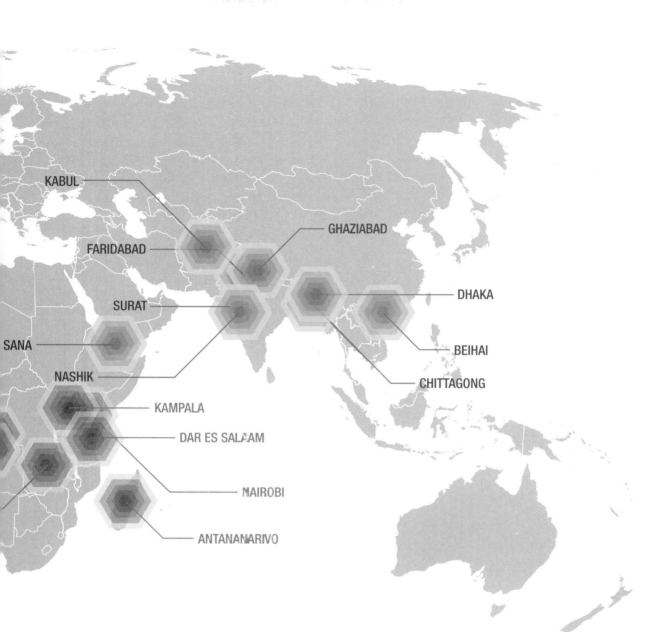

KABUL

GHAZIABAD

FARIDABAD

SURAT

DHAKA

SANA

NASHIK

BEIHAI

CHITTAGONG

KAMPALA

DAR ES SALAAM

NAIROBI

ANTANANARIVO

Currently, the average person in China emits less than a fifth of carbon dioxide into the atmosphere as the average American. But in 2007, China – with its 1.3 billion people – for the first time exceeded America as the world's largest overall emitter of carbon. What will happen when the average Chinese goes through the same amount of carbon as the typical American?

GROWING
CARBON EMISSIONS

Growth in metric tons of carbon dioxide emissions from 1994-2004.

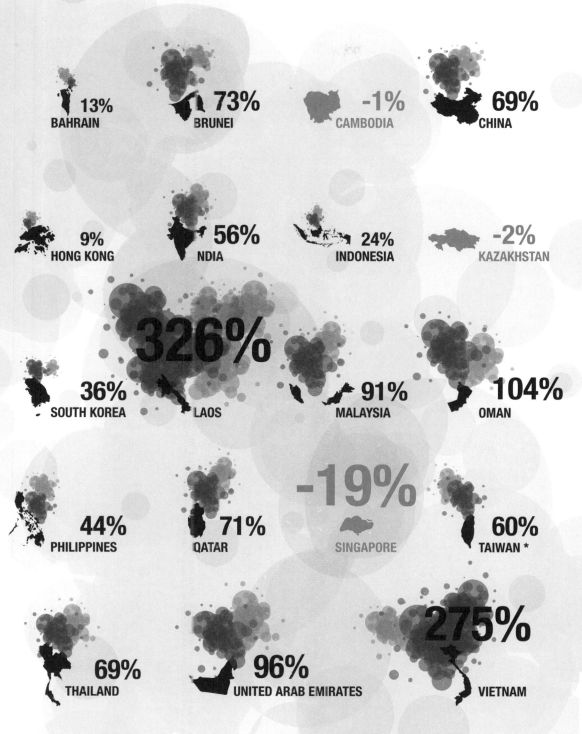

13%
BAHRAIN

73%
BRUNEI

-1%
CAMBODIA

69%
CHINA

9%
HONG KONG

56%
NDIA

24%
INDONESIA

-2%
KAZAKHSTAN

326%

36%
SOUTH KOREA

LAOS

91%
MALAYSIA

104%
OMAN

-19%
SINGAPORE

44%
PHILIPPINES

71%
QATAR

60%
TAIWAN *

275%

69%
THAILAND

96%
UNITED ARAB EMIRATES

VIETNAM

GROWING
CARBON EMISSIONS

Metric tons of carbon dioxide use per capita, 2004.

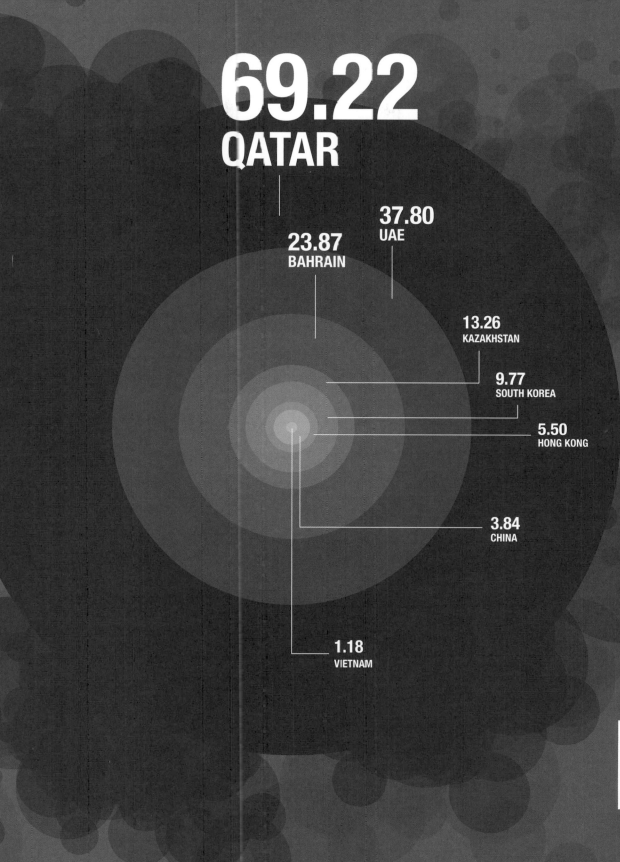

69.22
QATAR

37.80
UAE

23.87
BAHRAIN

13.26
KAZAKHSTAN

9.77
SOUTH KOREA

5.50
HONG KONG

3.84
CHINA

1.18
VIETNAM

Cars head towards the Avenue of Eternal Peace in Beijing's new Central Business District. Today, there are 3 million private vehicles registered in the city of Beijing. Five years ago, there were 800,000.

Power lines dot a desert landscape in the Emirates. Of the top ten countries with the highest per capita energy consumption, five are found on the Asian continent, including the top three.

According to the World Bank, sixteen of the world's twenty most polluted cities are in China, measured by particulate matter (PM) per cubic meter. The Chinese capital, Beijing, routinely has a PM rate in excess of 200. The World Health Organization classifies dangerous levels as a PM rate in excess of 50.

MAGIC MOUNTAINS

BY COBE ARCHITECTS

The cities of the emerging world are engaged in a frenzy of development that is scarring the land. Chongqing, the Sichuan city-county with a population of 31.7 million – of which more than 6 million live in a gritty urban core – exemplifies the growing urban footprint's impact on not just the land, but on surrounding air and water. The Copenhagen-based studio Cobe has proposed that rather than impose, Chongqing's growing umbra should fuse with the surrounding topography. By 2015, they envision this hilly city's extension will be a district of magic mountains – a place that echoes the land rather than conquers it. Meanwhile, millions of people can find home and work.

GREEN CBD 2015

Once you've been to Chongqing, it is hard to think of the city and not at the same time picture the beautiful mountains, and the majestic Yangtze River circumfloating the densely built Yuzhong Peninsula, only to absorb the waters of Jialing River just moments later. Where the yellow and the blue waters meet is the site for Chongqing's new "Green" Central Business District (GCBD).

We have designed the GCBD from a standpoint of sustainability – nevertheless in keeping with developers' demands and legal regulations.

We propose a pioneer project in which architectural and planning solutions reduce the overall consumption of resources and energy by 22%, whereby the GCBD will gain model status throughout Chongqing – where "the pace and scale of urbanization is faster and bigger than anywhere in the world today". (Guardian, March 15, 2006) IMAGINE! Chongqing could become China's green metropolis within 20 years by eliminating water, air and soil pollution, by stopping the trend of the ever increasing energy consumption and by reversing the rise of private car ownership!

Imagine, the Yangtze could be a clean river where swimming would no longer be a health risk – but again a test of courage for brave young men. Imagine, in 20 years the sun over Chongqing not be hidden behind a thick haze, but a sky of blue throughout the whole year!

Imagine 2015: Can you hear the birds sing? Can you feel the fresh breeze from the rivers? Can you see the green mountains at further distance? Shall we sing Mao's old song:

"I HAVE JUST DRUNK THE WATERS OF CHANGSHA AND COME TO EAT THE FISH OF WUCHANG, NOW I AM SWIMMING ACROSS THE GREAT YANGTZE, LOOKING AFAR TO THE OPEN SKY OF CHONGQING…"

(adopted after "Swimming", Mao Zedong)

HIGHSPEEDURBANISM

By 2015 the number of residents in metropolitan Chongqing will have doubled and 10 more million people will have moved from the fields to the new skyscrapers in downtown Chongqing. By the end of this decade 37 million people will be registered residents in Chongqing which is already now – with its 31.7 million inhabitants – is the biggest municipality worldwide.

In this highspeed development 50 million square meters of residential and commercial floor space, 500 kilometers of highways and almost two wide-span bridges are being added to the urban landscape every year. The annual 40% growth rate of Chongqing is higher than Shanghai's or Beijing's ever have been.

How can this boom be steered in a sustainable way so that the million times dream of prosperity does not exhaust the very resources needed to have a good life? *(according to official estimations)

Chongqing 2006 - 2015:
+ 1,200,000 people/year
+ 500 kilometers highway/year
+ 50,000,000 square meters/year
+ 17 new bridges
+ 3 airports

MOUNTAINOUS CITY

Chongqing is a mountainous city. Fertile, arable land and human habitation are limited to the lower river valleys. These also constitute the prime locations for Chongqing's future growth. However, most of this land is already urbanized. Furthermore, large areas of this habitat may be flooded as a consequence of the Three Gorges Project.

Land is especially scarce in metropolitan Chongqing. Most of the area that is easily accessible is already under heavy use. The few available reserves have been dedicated as building sites to partially accommodate the growth up until 2015. However, the main strategy for meeting the future demands lies in the intensification of the use of the land and to increase the urban density in metropolitan Chongqing – there is no room for sprawl!

As a result of the densification, the newly built "wall of high-rises" is not only blocking the visual connection with the surrounding mountains – it also threatens to blur the city's unique image as a mountainous city. Furthermore, in ten years from now there will be only few buildings left in Chongqing constructed before 1980 (Spiegel, December 16, 2005).

Why can't landscape become a valuable element of identification when much of the built heritage is lost?

EXHAUSTED CITY

One does not need to be an alarmist to acknowledge that the immense speed in which Chongqing is growing might soon stretch the limits of the city's resources.

The architectural production of the city is immense: in the current highspeed development 50 million square meters of buildings are constructed

AMOUNT OF UNRECYCLED TRASH DISCARDED IN THE CITY DURING 10 YEARS: APPROXIMATELY
12.7 MILLION TONNES.

in the city every year. That equals the completion of three Chrysler buildings every other day. The few central and easily accessible land reserves in the lower mountain reaches will soon be exhausted.

3500 tons of waste are discarded in the city every day – only little is recycled or incinerated. The Yangtze is the most polluted river in China because untreated wastewater from the industries and households of 186 cities is discharged into it. One of these cities is Chongqing. Because most of the power used in Chongqing comes from burning fossil fuels and inadequate exhaust treatment facilities, clean air is a luxury and the city is suffering from acid rain.

Like everywhere else in China, living standards in Chongqing are increasing by the day and the rate of private car ownership is doubling every five years.

How can Chongqing proceed with its ambitious project to improve the living conditions of 37 million people without exhausting the very resources needed to sustain the better life (adopted from UID)?

2003: Municipality of Chongqing

2015: Metropolitan Chongqing

2003: Metropolitan Chongqing

2015: New building land and densification

2015: IF CHINA HAS THE STRENGTH AND CAPACITY TO GENERATE 84 BILLION KWH PER YEAR – CAN THEN NOT ALSO THE EQUIVALENT BE SAVED AS THE NEXT STEP TOWARDS SUSTAINABLE URBAN DEVELOPMENT?

ELECTRIC CITY

With the "Three Gorges Project" (TGP), Chongqing is the location of one of the most controversially debated construction projects worldwide. Even though the retaining wall of the dam is situated in the neighbouring province of Hubei, 80% of the impact area of the mega-project is located in Chongqing (Hartmann, 2002).

The TGP was launched in 1993 and was completed in 2008 – one year ahead of schedule. It comprises an 800 kilometers long water reservoir with a 2,300 meters long and 200 meters high retaining wall. It is the largest hydroelectric dam ever constructed – planned to provide the prosperous cities in the east and southeast with energy.

As a consequence of the rising water level, 13 cities, 140 towns and 1352 villages will be "submerged" under the water and 1,2 million people resettled by 2008 – 85% of them being from Chongqing (Three Gorges Information Centre, 2005).

Following completion, a total of 84 billion kWh/year will be generated. That equals 11-15% of China's energy demand. The costs are officially estimated at 25 billion US$ (Three Gorges Information Centre, 2005).

Imagine! China has the strength and capacity to generate so much energy – can then the country not also save the equivalent as the next step towards sustainable urban development?

MAGIC MOUNTAINS

The urban concept for the GCBD reinstates the mountainous feeling deep into the very dense and urbanized areas of Chongqing. The new skyline consists of a composition of inhabited mountains. The mountain peaks match the high-density centers; the lower reaches of the mountains resemble areas built with low density, whereas the valleys are green open spaces.

The mountains are a response to what Chongqing today is all about: The contemporary high-rise city is eating up the cultural and architectural heritage of Chongqing, open green spaces and traditional neighbourhoods.

The mountain skyline will become the symbol of Chongqing's new identity as China's green metropolis. It functions as a pioneer of the dawning change from explosive highspeedurbanism to a soft green urban revolution.

THE LIVING MACHINE

According to Chongqing's regulation plan, the 2.2 square kilometers site for Chongqing's new green CBD has a capacity of 15.4 million square meters floor space – that equals a floor area ratio of 7 (FAR = 7). We think of this high urban density as a tool for accommodating the immense demand for housing and offices under severe space constraints and market pressure. However, the density in itself does not provide a sufficient sustainable answer to the highspeed challenges! We therefore suggest the reservation of 1/3 of the area for the integration of an ecological chain in which production, consumption, waste, and circulation are linked with the aim of less pollution, high energy efficiency and low energy input – the living machine.

To realize the site's building potential of 15.4 million square meters and to balance the loss of valuable square meters, the density in the remaining 2/3 of the area has to be increased to FAR = 10.

On an urban scale the living machine complements the demands for high density with low density qualities of traditional Chinese neighbourhoods – open green spaces, fresh air, lively street atmosphere. On an architectural scale, the living machine integrates low-tech solutions for the high-tech demands of the highspeedurbanism.

The regulation plan for the CBD suggests 60% office space, 25% housing and 15% for commercial, social and leisure facilities. We suggest a dedication of 5% of the program to sustainable facilities, such as wind turbines or wastewater treatment facilities. All of these will be integrated into the living machine.

FIVE MINUTES CITY

In this GCBD everything is reachable within a five walking distance: the next public transport stop, cultural/commercial/social institutions and a park or green space.

The urban layout radically promotes walking, cycling and the use of public transport – it deliberately excludes cars. A state of the art monorail spine links the site on a regional level to the "old" and the other planned CBD across the rivers, as well as to the airport and the new central station.

A 5.5 kilometers long loop ensures fast and easy transit within the mini-city. Monorail stops are located in the densest centers of the nine neighbourhoods. Every point within the site is within five minutes walking distance of the monorail stops.

An additional monorail line connects stops in the living machine with the stations in the urban centers. This line brings people to the social and cultural amenities or the riverbanks in a fast and efficient way.

LOW-TECH PRINCIPLES

1 Green Mountains
Because the site is not sealed for motorized traffic, up to 95% of the entire surface can be used to "bring back the trees". Even on the terraced roof spaces of each building huge

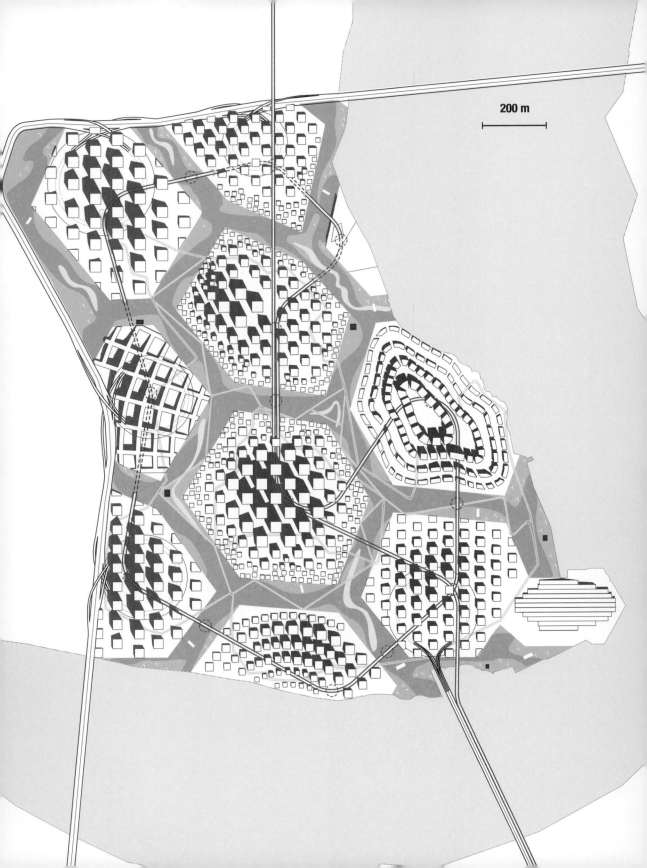

200 m

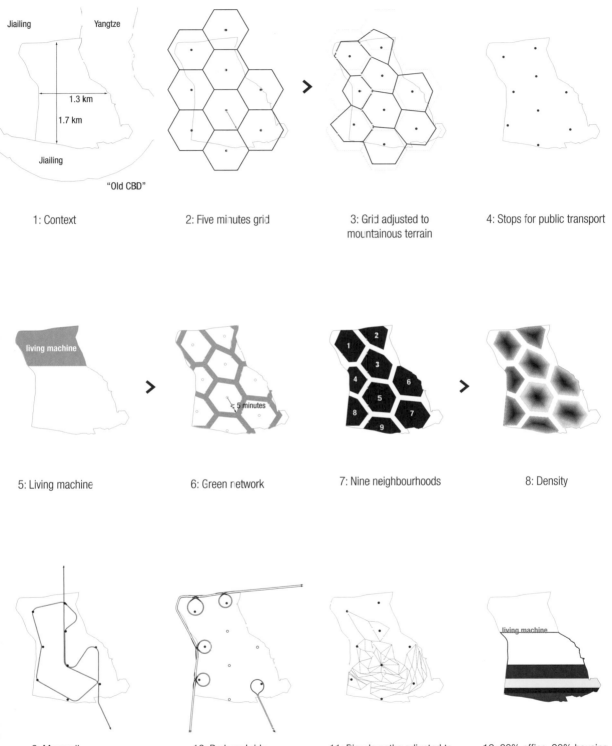

1: Context

2: Five minutes grid

3: Grid adjusted to mountainous terrain

4: Stops for public transport

5: Living machine

6: Green network

7: Nine neighbourhoods

8: Density

9: Monorail

10: Park and ride

11: Bicycle paths adjusted to mountainous terrain

12: 60% office, 20% housing, 12 % commercial, 8% hotel, 10% leisure areas of greenery can be planted. This strategy not only creates high quality outdoor spaces – it also helps in considerably reducing the carbon footprint of the area.

2 Underground Root Zone
An underground root zone system is constructed underneath the entire living machine. This system cleans all the wastewater from the area. Every day this 0.75 km^2 ecological system can clean almost all of the wastewater. This will allow us to re-introduce clean water to the Yangtze and Jialing Rivers and hence contribute to their ecological restoration.

3 Breeze Valleys
The urban layout supports natural ventilation and the generation of wind energy: The orientation of the valleys between the green mountains is optimized to catch the cooling winds from the rivers and the north in summer time. Where the stronger winds from the north enter the area small-scale windmills are positioned to create renewable energy within the GCBD. This energy is used for illuminating the park areas during night and to serve the public facilities with power. The windmills are designed as decorative wind lights.

4 Solar Catcher
The cluster with the biggest surface is optimized to catch solar energy throughout the entire day. In this neighbourhood all roof areas are mounted with solar panels, which will generate enough warm water for all of the buildings in the GCBD. The "golden mountain" becomes a new landmark for Chongqing.

5 Golden Wind
Drawing from vernacular Chinese architecture, natural ventilation will be incorporated in the design of each individual building. In summer time, pagoda style roofs can screen from the harsh sunlight and catch the rolling winds to passively cool the buildings. Wind cuts and hollow ceilings allow the winds to float through each level. Because no cars are allowed in the GCBD, a fresh breeze is blowing from the rivers, and the green mountains produce a lot of oxygen, the air is good enough to open the windows! The golden wind strategy not only helps reduce the demand for electricity by cutting air conditioning, it also helps each office and housing unit increase their disposable income by reducing their energy bill!

6 Proximity Points
The five minute city is a strategy for a car free district where walking, cycling and the use of public transport is the most convenient way of getting around. Instead of supporting individual motorized transport we provide each of the nine individual neighbourhoods with a state-of-the-art monorail station in their densest center. The urban layout is such that residents and visitors can reach any point in the area within a five minute walking distance from a monorail stop.

Additional stations on the continuous green park take people to the social and cultural amenities or the riverbanks in a fast and efficient way.

7 Context Sensitive Design
While some of the sustainable solutions are generic, for example the reduction of car transport, some

of the proposed solutions can only be implemented in relation to the local climatic and geographic conditions or the demands of the program.

Buildings along the highway for example can function as noise barriers. Others can be optimized according to sun and wind conditions.

8 Money For Trash

We suggest the introduction of a waste recycling system where resource waste can be traded for money. The residents are to have the opportunity to return their waste back into the resource cycle in a convenient way. Collection points for the waste recycling system will be located at prominent nodes in the living machine.

5 PRINCIPLES OF HOW TO BUILD A SUSTAINABLE CITY

When the grey haze in front of the sun lifts, we can anticipate the bright future we would like to live in. We imagine cities built on radically green designs, sustainable energy, and non-toxic recyclable materials. Market forces and political power will help to propel us into the green future – there is no other responsible alternative! Our design for a Green Central Business District is guided by five very simple principles, which together can make a sustainable city.

1 The Future Belongs To The Cities!
Sprawl eats land and puts stress on the ecosystem by increasing the need for transportation – be it individual or public. Planners can make better use of space, energy and public investments by placing buildings, different functions and nature close to each other. This will promote walking, cycling, public transit and foster community.

2 Energy Efficiency Creates Value
Waste is costly in all imaginable dimensions. Consuming less water, power and materials is cheaper! Well-insulated, naturally ventilated buildings full of natural light will help their users waste less energy. Power-saving appliances will pay for themselves in the long run.

3 Renewable Energy Is Abundant Energy
The use of conventional energies comes at high costs; and the resources are not end-less. Renewable alternatives promise clean energy: wind turbines, solar arrays, wave power units small-scale hydro-electric generators, or geothermal systems. There is no responsible alternative to not integrating these solutions wherever possible!

4 Quality Is Wealth
More is not better – but better is better! People do not need bigger apartments – they need different floor plans. People do not need bigger cars – they need better cycle paths or public transport! People do not need more stuff to throw away – they need quality that will last!

5 Closed Loop City
Every neighbourhood, urban district and city needs to be conceived as a "cycling economy" where production, consumption, waste and circulation are understood as an integrated ecological chain.

1,000,000,000
ASIANS GAINED ACCESS TO DRINKING WATER IN THE PERIOD FROM 1990 TO 2004

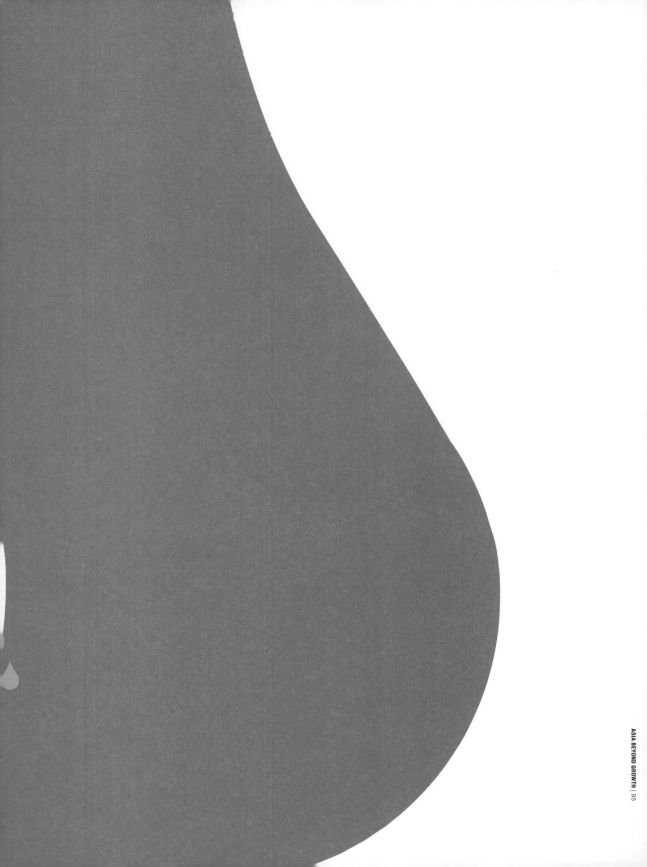

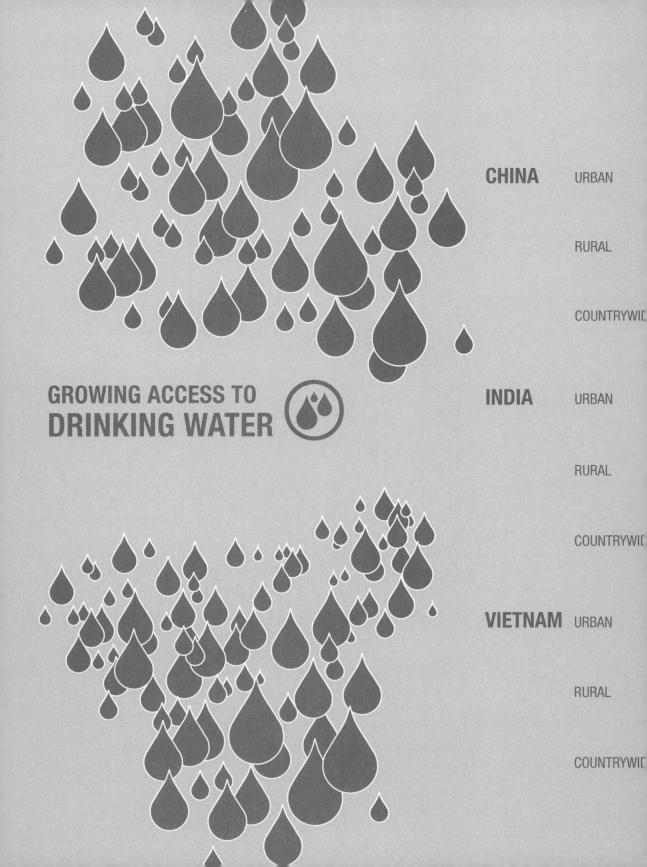

GROWING ACCESS TO
DRINKING WATER

CHINA   URBAN

            RURAL

            COUNTRYWID

INDIA   URBAN

            RURAL

            COUNTRYWID

VIETNAM   URBAN

            RURAL

            COUNTRYWID

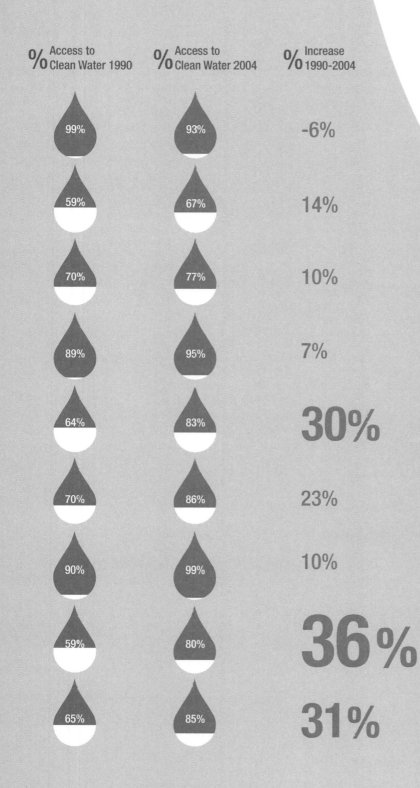

% Access to Clean Water 1990
% Access to Clean Water 2004
% Increase 1990-2004

Access to Clean Water 1990	Access to Clean Water 2004	Increase 1990-2004
99%	93%	-6%
59%	67%	14%
70%	77%	10%
89%	95%	7%
64%	83%	30%
70%	86%	23%
90%	99%	10%
59%	80%	36%
65%	85%	31%

GROWING
SANITATION

Percentage increase in those
with access to adequate sanitation
in the period from 1994-2004.

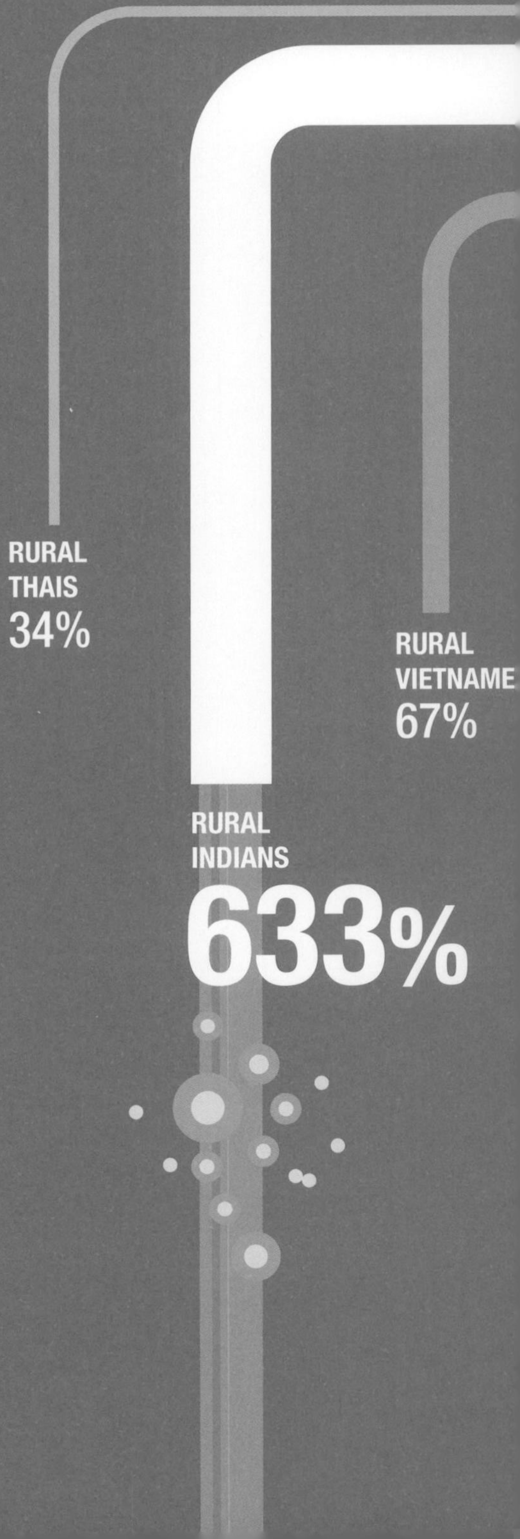

**RURAL
THAIS
34%**

**RURAL
VIETNAME
67%**

**RURAL
INDIANS**

633%

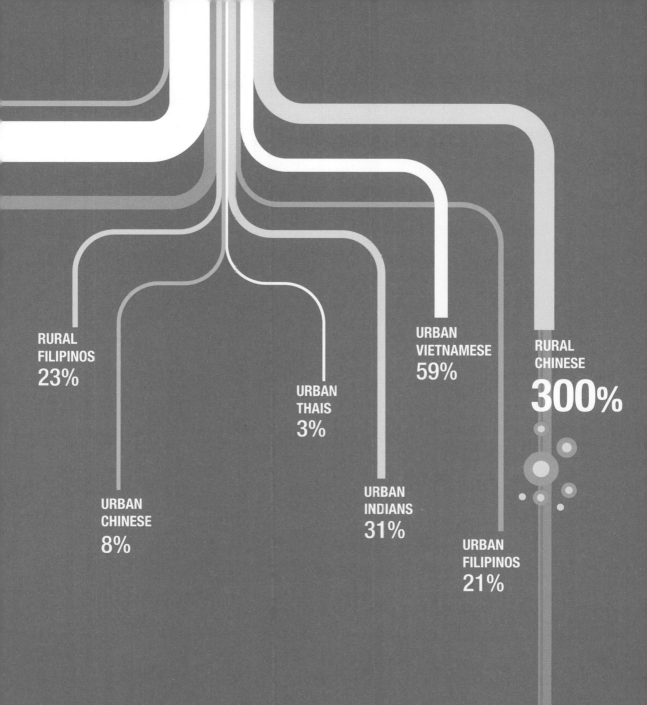

RURAL
FILIPINOS
23%

URBAN
THAIS
3%

URBAN
VIETNAMESE
59%

RURAL
CHINESE
300%

URBAN
CHINESE
8%

URBAN
INDIANS
31%

URBAN
FILIPINOS
21%

While only one in three rural Chinese today has access to adequate sanitation, it still represents a tripling in the number from twenty years ago.

Improved access to and awareness of sanitation has been one of the biggest benefits of Asia's economic development. From left to right, a child urinates in a Beijing alleyway, a public toilet in Beijing, and a public toilet (designed by us) at Dragon Lake Park in Bengbu, China.

FROM WASTELAND TO PARKLAND: EDAW TURNS SHANGHAI INDUSTRIAL PARK FROM GREY TO GREEN

China's leading economic and commercial center has invested more and more money in pollution control while maintaining rapid economic development in recent years.

And we have been an integral part of that effort with its recent transformation of the massively polluted Shanghai Chemical Industrial Park into a thriving, vibrant parkland.

THE UNIQUE CHARACTERISTICS OF THE WASTEWATER REQUIRE A RIGOROUSLY ENGINEERED APPROACH TOWARDS IMPROVING WATER QUALITY, AND OUR MASTER PLAN, A TREATMENT WETLAND WITH MULTIPLE PROGRAMS, IS A FIRST FOR CHINA.

Located southeast of Shanghai on the coast of Hangzhou Bay, the Shanghai Chemical Industrial Park (SCIP) consists of more than a dozen modern petrochemical facilities. The site's steward, the Shanghai Chemical Industry Park Administration Committee, presented us with a brief calling for a water treatment system that would purify industrial wastewater effluent for recycling within the industrial park and for discharge into Hangzhou Bay. The result is a sensitive park that offers a way forward for the mitigation of environment trauma to the burgeoning Asian cityscape.

OUR ECOLOGICAL VISION
We envisioned a 30 hectare Natural Wastewater Treatment System that would treat over 22,000 cube meters/day of partially-treated industrial wastewater.

We recognized the potential to further treat the effluent in a Natural Treatment System, which included the provisioning of a constructed wetland – a productive landscape that would also be a new public space. The polished, or now cleansed and treated, wastewater would provide a source of clean water for on-site water features, have the potential to be reused in various industrial processes, and will further protect the coastal ecology of Hangzhou Bay.

TECHNICAL SOLUTIONS
Key technical aims of the project were to improve effluent from the industrial

WHILE MANAGING WATER QUALITY WAS A KEY PRIORITY, OUR COLLABORATION BROUGHT TOGETHER LANDSCAPE ARCHITECTS AND ECOLOGISTS CREATING A DISTINCT AESTHETIC WHILE INTRODUCING WILDLIFE HABITATS.

wastewater treatment plant to comply with groundwater and soil standards and to prevent toxicity in the treatment system.

While managing water quality was a key priority, our collaboration brought together landscape architects and ecologists creating a distinct aesthetic while introducing wildlife habitats.

The treatment system is thus more than just that, it is a recreational hub, and a living bio-habitat set within the chaotic growth of metropolitan Shanghai.

Realizing this vision and its objectives required practical solutions for a host of issues and challenges related to the site conditions and quality of the effluent wastewater. After extensive discuss on between us and professionals from Shanghai's Tongji University and the University of California, Berkeley, an innovative natural filter system was developed that removed chemical pollutants from the site.

THE DESIGN MOVES BEYOND THE RHYTHMS OF MECHANICAL TREATMENT, AND HAS PEOPLE AND AESTHETICS VERY MUCH IN MIND, IN ORDER TO CREATE A PLACE THAT IS MORE THAN A TREATMENT AREA, BUT A TRUE PUBLIC PARK THAT ADDS TRUE SPATIAL VALUE TO WHAT IS OTHERWISE A GRITTY CONTEXT SCARRED BY INDUSTRIAL POLLUTION.

上海化学工业区

This provided the basis for our master plan, which included three main treatment components: A Trickling Filter in which built towers remove ammonia from water that passes through, two 7,300 square meters ponds that degrade carbon dioxide, and a 22 hectare free surface wetland with built-in parallel treatment systems.

HUMANISTIC ELEMENTS EMPHASIZED

It is in this spirit that a small visitor's center is an inspirational component of the master plan; this is accompanied by a plant wetland, an isolated island habitat for birds and intertwined boardwalks that allow for and encourage visitor access. We also programmed seven research wetland cells to be located near the site's southern entrance that help monitors to gage the Park's overall effectiveness. Regional and local plant species were sought, with aesthetic considerations also playing a role in selection, in order to help convey a more naturalistic tone.

FUTURE MODEL

The Shanghai Chemical Industrial Park is not only the first of its kind to be designed by us, but is a similarly unique project for China, marking the onset of what could be a model for future productive landscapes for rapidly growing Chinese and developing cities.

WHILE THE IMPROVEMENT OF WATER QUALITY IS SYSTEMATICALLY ADDRESSED IN THIS UNIQUE DESIGN, EDAW'S FUSION OF DISCIPLINES ALLOWED THE TREATMENT WETLANDS TO EVOLVE INTO AN ATTRACTIVE NATURAL ENVIRONMENT SUITABLE FOR BOTH WILDLIFE HABITATS AND VISITORS.

TODAY, THERE ARE MORE THAN
3,700,000 SQUARE KILOMETERS OF PROTECTED LAND IN ASIA,
WHICH IS ROUGHLY THE EQUIVALENT TO THE LAND AREA OF ALL OF INDIA.

HOW MUCH MORE WILL BE NEEDED TO PROTECT THE 4,500 ENDANGERED SPECIES CURRENTLY STRUGGLING TO SURVIVE ON THE CONTINENT?

DISAPPEARING
SPECIES

Increase in number of species classified as endangered in the period from 1990-2004.

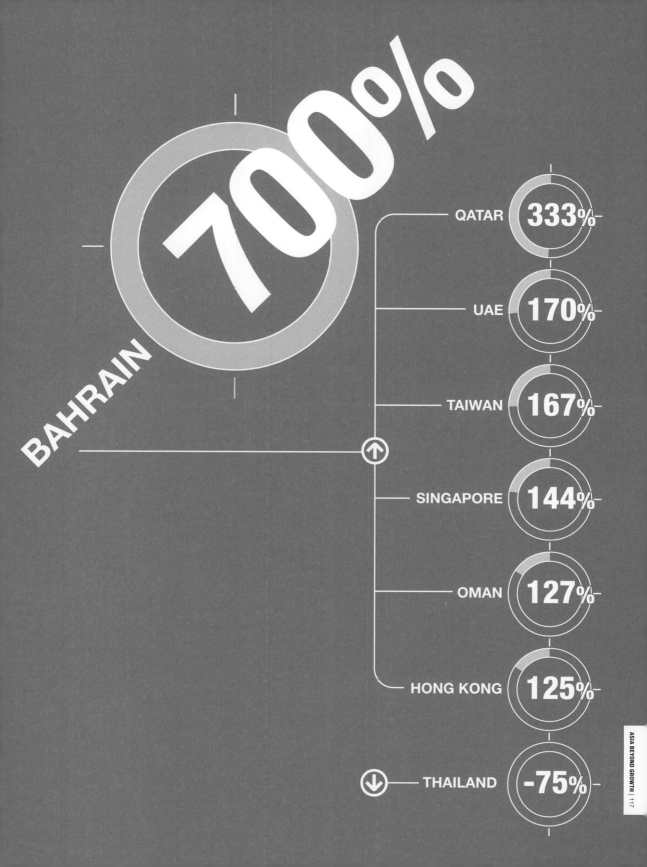

700%

BAHRAIN

QATAR 333%

UAE 170%

TAIWAN 167%

SINGAPORE 144%

OMAN 127%

HONG KONG 125%

THAILAND -75%

GROWING
PROTECTION

Percentage growth in total protected area in the period from 1990-2004.

27,6

CAMBODIA
37,385%

QATAR
3%

BAHRAIN
606%

UAE
1,401%

LAOS
1,669%

PHILIPPINES
63%

VIETNAM
287%

THAILAND
46%

INDONESIA
37%

GROWING
FORESTED LAND

Percentage change in forested land in the period from 1990-2005.

BAHRAIN
107%

VIETNAM
37%

UAE
27%

CHINA
26%

IND
6%

DECLINING
FORESTED LAND

INDONESIA
-24%

CAMBODIA
-19%

LAOS
-7%

MALAYSIA
-7%

SHENZHEN DISCOVERS ITS NATURAL BEAUTY

Coastlines are ever more sought after commodities in the climate of economic upsurge in China. In this project, we considered a new typology, providing a sustainable framework to establish a long term strategy for local statutory planning on one of the largest remaining (258 square kilometers) contiguous natural coastline areas in Southern China. Our vision responds to Shenzhen's hyper-urbanization in the last 20 years – evolving from a migrant city to an emerging, livable international coastal city.

BACKGROUND

Shenzhen's physical and economic connectivity with Hong Kong, once the main driver behind the decision to make the city a special economic zone in Mainland China, has been gradually shifting away from the singular economic focus of a global manufacturing hub. With that in mind, we were asked to look at the last remaining natural area within that zone. With approximately 150 kilometers of coastline that comprises one-eighth of the total area within the city limits of Shenzhen, the city government was envisioning a new leisure experience of coastal parks as an alternate 'getaway' for the new social structure of established immigrants within the city.

The unique and varied topography and geology supports a high diversity of animal and plant habitats, and there is evidence of volcanic activities dating from 140 million years ago. Meanwhile, the area has also been experiencing development pressure with construction

CONTRARY TO THE PRECONCEIVED IMPRESSION OF CONTEMPORARY SHENZHEN'S URBANITY, THE STUDY AREA CAN BE CONSIDERED 'PRISTINE' BY ANY STANDARDS, CONTAINING 23 NATURAL SANDY BEACHES, LARGE MOUNTAIN RANGES, REGIONALLY SIGNIFICANT FOREST HABITATS, WETLANDS, AS WELL AS TRADITIONAL AGRICULTURAL AND FISHING VILLAGE SETTINGS.

of new expressways and power lines, and the
intensification of Shenzhen's urban sprawl.

PURPOSE

With an initial understanding of the scale and
environmental complexities, we were successful
in persuading the city's Coastal Planning Bureau
to approach the study area from the initial overall
perspective of resource management. We
departed from the original brief, which simply
asked for the identification and planning of an
independent Coastal Park System purely on the
bases of supporting future recreational needs.

The broadened scope includes review and
analysis of all of the natural and cultural
resources present in the subject area. The
degree or level of integration between
environmental and developmental concerns
became the guiding framework for the coastal
park system, future developments, circulation
networks and conservation reserves collectively.
To this end, the study broadly consists of
two components: 1) a resource analysis and
development of environmental recommendations
and guidelines, and 2) a coastal park master plan.

Data for Geographic Information System (GIS)
mapping was gathered through extensive
collaborations with local communities. This
resource analytical tool enabled the redefinition
of the boundaries of a statutory 'eco-line'
and began to define resources as a series
of integrated influx systems. The introduction
of GIS was intended as an act of knowledge
transfer that provided a new platform allowing
local authorities to manage their natural and
cultural resources beyond the duration of the
project life.

Enjoyment of nature is usually associated only
within existing designated tourist destinations
in China. In this sense, the project objective
of creating a comprehensive outdoor country
park system for leisure and hiking would be
considered unique. The intention here was
to create a framework for a country park system
that draws upon the localized environmental,
scenic and cultural qualities while taking into
consideration future developments and visitors'
needs. Circulation via trails, cycle routes and
water would connect different open spaces
of various landscape qualities to serve
recreational and educational needs.

RESOURCE ANALYSIS & ENVIRONMENTAL RECOMMENDATIONS

Our site understanding drew upon collaboration
with local experts, including local professionals,
hikers, academics and environmental groups
through six months of detailed field investigations.
Existing land and marine resources were

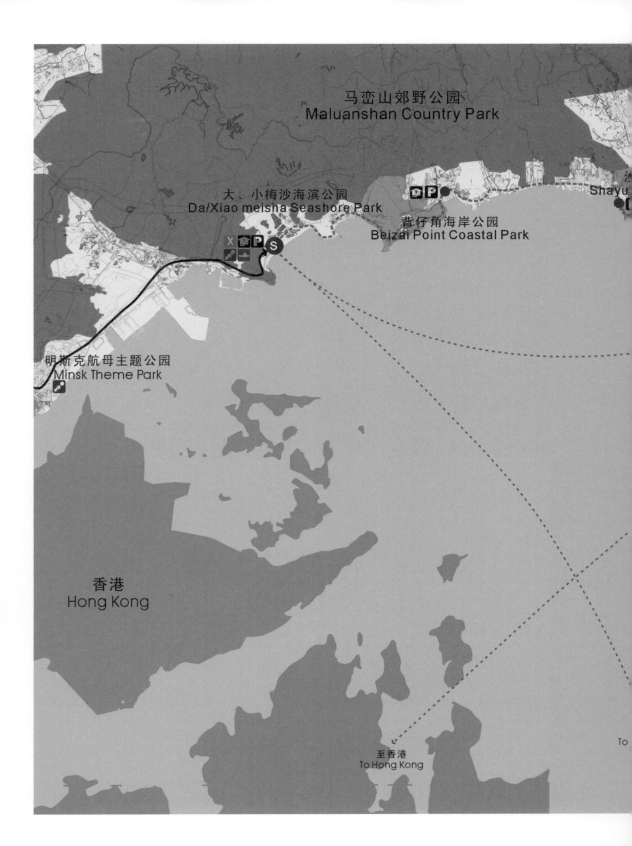

马峦山郊野公园
Maluanshan Country Park

大、小梅沙海滨公园
Da/Xiao meisha Seashore Park

背仔角海岸公园
Beizai Point Coastal Park

Shayu

明斯克航母主题公园
Minsk Theme Park

香港
Hong Kong

至香港
To Hong Kong

To

坝光湿地
Baguang Wetland

排牙山郊野公园
Paiyashan Country Park

海岸公园
...oastal Park

大鹏古城
Dapeng

雀山海岸公园
Que Shan Coastal

下沙海滨公园
Xiasha Seashore Park

东山海岸公园
Dongshan Coastal Park

杨梅坑
Yangmeikeng

高甲角
Gaojiajiao

南澳海岸公园
Nanao Coastal Park

七娘山 869米
Mount Qiniang 869M

大燕顶 801米

七娘山国家地质公园
Qiniangshan National Park

三角山 658米

海柴
Haicho...

洋筹角
Yangchou Point

东冲
Dongchong

鹅公湾
Egong Bay

东西冲海岸公园
Dongxichong Coastal Park

红花岭 379米
Honghualing

西冲
Xichong

穿鼻岩
Chuanbiyan

大鹿湾
Dalu Bay

尖峰顶 390米
Jianfeng Top

赖氏洲
Laishi Island

catalogued; in particular we looked at changes of the visual landscape by recent development perceived both from inland and from water.

LOCAL VILLAGERS AND TOURISTS ALIKE WERE INTERVIEWED SO THE PLANNING TEAM COULD BETTER UNDERSTAND THE VERNACULAR CHARACTER OF THE INDIGENOUS HUMAN CULTURE, AND THE EXPECTATIONS OF LOCAL VISITORS.

Field investigations were coupled with extensive use of remote sensing data including satellite imagery, aerial photography, historical and current land-use plans to gain a multi-dimensional understanding of the area. The result was an integrated GIS-based inventory that included assessments of the area's biological, geological and water resources, agricultural and cultural resources, as well as areas that had endured environmental degradation caused by agriculture and aquaculture, which were highlighted for ecological remediation. Using this, we were able to determine composite resource sensitivity and overall development suitability, which were used as a knowledge transfer to local authorities to allow them to evaluate the integral relationship between different conservation degrees and different intensities of development.

The study reviewed the city's own system of natural preservation and cross-checked these boundaries with the integrated GIS findings regarding environmentally sensitive areas. These findings helped to readjust the official boundaries of a protected "eco-line" to expand the protection buffer of environmentally-sensitive habitats, which were not conferred protection under the present system. This new line was particularly relevant for the protection of inter-tidal areas of mudflats with established mangrove forests. The redefinition of the eco-line increased the protected area by over 1500 hectares in pockets ranging from 10 - 180 hectares.

COASTAL PARK MASTER PLAN
Following the environmental analysis, the coastal park system was developed in conjunction

with existing transport infrastructure and connections, scenic and landscape values, development capacities as well as a review of the city's overall planning strategy vis-à-vis the area. Studies on visitation and traffic capacity, landscape nodes and activities, and recommendations for future park management were conducted. Central to this was to decide how to preserve existing environments while also introducing new areas for recreational uses, as well as the accommodation of land allocation for development given the city's inevitable eastward expansion.

The working definition of the proposed coastal park system was a continuous natural shoreline of certain ecological value with a depth less than 2 kilometers of scenic and recreational value that existed for the public's outdoor enjoyment. This was adopted as a general definition to differentiate from the established statutory comprehensive open space system. This helped to initiate a park management resource strategy that differed from common urban parks.

Together with scenic reserves, country parks (including a forest park), wetlands (preserved and wetland park), they form an ecological open space system. This potentially would have a wider impact and critical wildlife connection within the Pearl River Delta region.

Through the development of the coastal park master plan, three key nodes were identified strategically to serve as potential pilot park projects while together serving as catalysts for other types of developments within the

THE SYSTEM OF COASTAL PARKS WAS PLANNED NOT ONLY AS A PLACE FOR RECREATION AND ENVIRONMENTAL PROTECTION, BUT ALSO AS A 'HONEYPOT' TO DRAW PEOPLE AWAY FROM THE OVERALL SITE'S MORE ECOLOGICALLY SENSITIVE AREAS, RATHER THAN CONSUMING AND IMPACTING THE PROTECTED MOUNTAINS, FORESTS AND OTHER NATURAL RESOURCES.

study area. These parks, ranging in size from 200-950 hectares, provide different experiences from family oriented resort setting, sports recreation to natural/scenic. The planning framework of each destination ensured that the natural assets of each local area were both capitalized on and protected while devising different strategies for future regional connectivity and park management.

As continuation to the study, we are now assisting the local authorities in the detail planning of a 16 kilometer-long coastal scenic drive as indicated in the proposed master plan as part of an 'experiential' infrastructure that supports the agreed-to development potential. These open spaces and protected areas dominate a large part of Shenzhen's east coast study zone and the study is not intended to be finite. The master plan identifies the key principles of an ecologically sensitive planning approach and arms the city with technical know-how through knowledge-transfer so that it can better anticipate changes in time. But for now, one can see that Shenzhen is making a right turn towards progressive planning while continuously moving forward as an emerging international city. The creation of a coastal park system is profoundly progessive one for a Chinese municipality.

THE CREATION OF A NEW SYSTEM OF COUNTRY PARKS AND ECOLOGICAL RESERVES IS A PROFOUNDLY PROGRESSIVE ONE FOR CHINA.

GROWTH: VERTICA

VS HORIZONTAL

SHANGH

MUMB

DUB

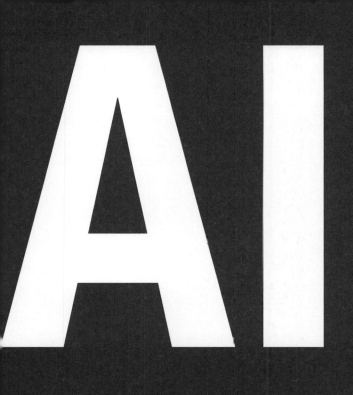

THE EMERGING WORLD IS AN ARC OF GROWTH FROM SHANGHAI TO MUMBAI TO DUBAI.

DUI

MUMB

SHANGH

SHANGHAI

Urban land area: **6,340 square kilometers**   Size of economy: **US$177.15 billion**
Density: **2,621 per square kilometers**

MUMBAI

Urban land area: **950 square kilometers**   Size of economy: **US$207.8 billion**
Density: **21,880 per square kilometers**

DUBAI

Urban land area: **1,287.4 square kilometers** Size of economy: **US$55 billion**
Density: **408.1 per square kilometers**

16 OF THE WORLD'S 20 TALLEST BUILDINGS CURRENTLY BUILT OR UNDER CONSTRUCTION CAN BE FOUND IN ASIA

20 YEARS AGO, 19 OF THE TOP 20 WERE IN NORTH AMERICA

MOSCOW

CHICAGO

NEW YORK

TOWERING AMBITIONS

Location of the world's 20 tallest buildings by 2010.

MEC

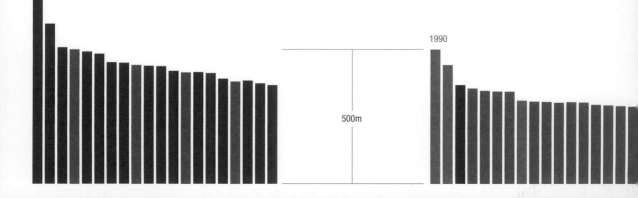

2010

1990

500m

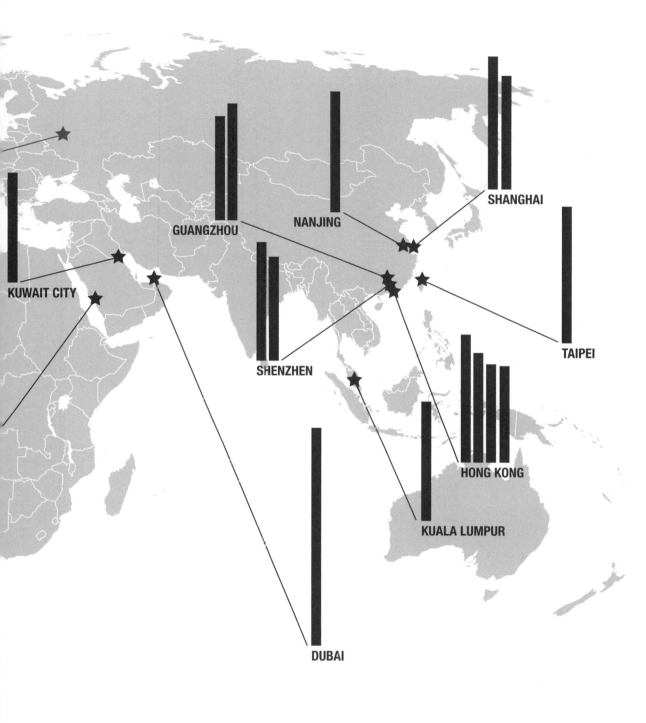

KUWAIT CITY

GUANGZHOU

NANJING

SHANGHAI

TAIPEI

SHENZHEN

HONG KONG

KUALA LUMPUR

DUBAI

EW

NON-EW

SKYSCRAPERS
SHANGHAI

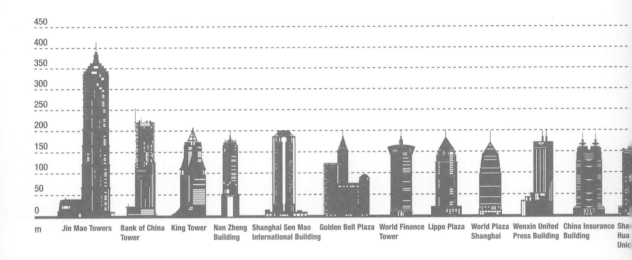

450
400
350
300
250
200
150
100
50
0
m

Jin Mao Towers | Bank of China Tower | King Tower | Nan Zheng Building | Shanghai Sen Mao International Building | Golden Bell Plaza | World Finance Tower | Lippo Plaza | World Plaza Shanghai | Wenxin United Press Building | China Insurance Building | Sha Hua Unic

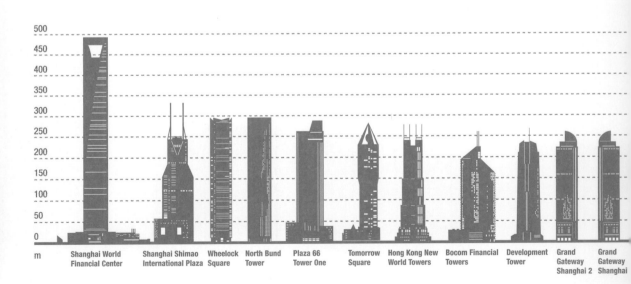

500
450
400
350
300
250
200
150
100
50
0
m

Shanghai World Financial Center | Shanghai Shimao International Plaza | Wheelock Square | North Bund Tower | Plaza 66 Tower One | Tomorrow Square | Hong Kong New World Towers | Bocom Financial Towers | Development Tower | Grand Gateway Shanghai 2 | Grand Gateway Shanghai

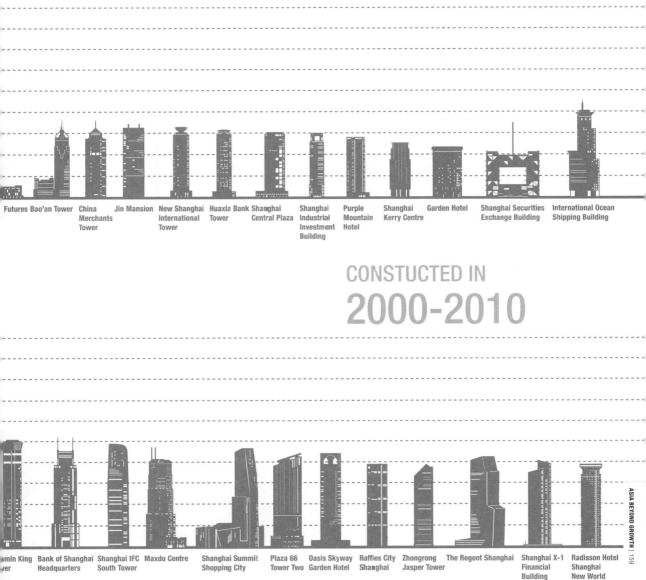

Futures Bao'an Tower | China Merchants Tower | Jin Mansion | New Shanghai International Tower | Huaxia Tower | Bank Shanghai Central Plaza | Shanghai Industrial Investment Building | Purple Mountain Hotel | Shanghai Kerry Centre | Garden Hotel | Shanghai Securities Exchange Building | International Ocean Shipping Building

min King er | Bank of Shanghai Headquarters | Shanghai IFC South Tower | Maxdo Centre | Shanghai Summit Shopping City | Plaza 66 Tower Two | Oasis Skyway Garden Hotel | Raffles City Shanghai | Zhongrong Jasper Tower | The Regent Shanghai | Shanghai X-1 Financial Building | Radisson Hotel Shanghai New World

SKYSCRAPERS
MUMBAI

1988

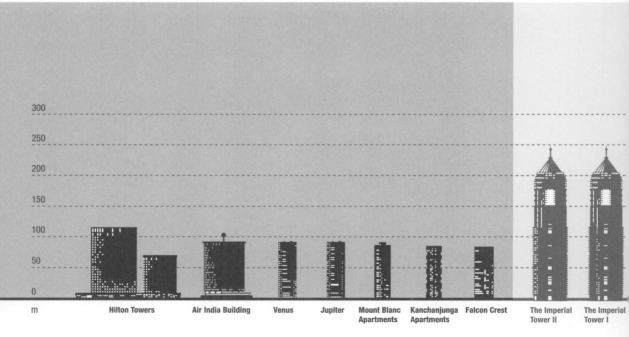

m Hilton Towers   Air India Building   Venus   Jupiter   Mount Blanc Apartments   Kanchanjunga Apartments   Falcon Crest   The Imperial Tower II   The Imperial Tower I

2007

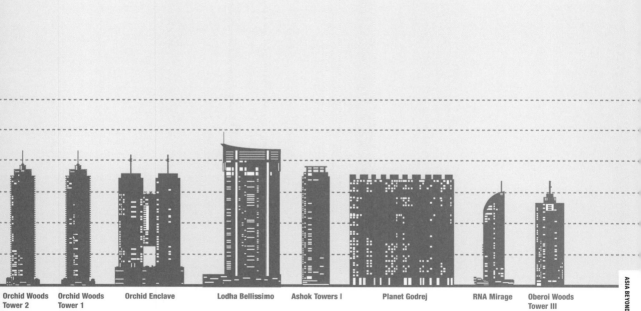

Orchid Woods
Tower 2

Orchid Woods
Tower 1

Orchid Enclave

Lodha Bellissimo

Ashok Towers I

Planet Godrej

RNA Mirage

Oberoi Woods
Tower III

SKYSCRAPERS
DUBAI

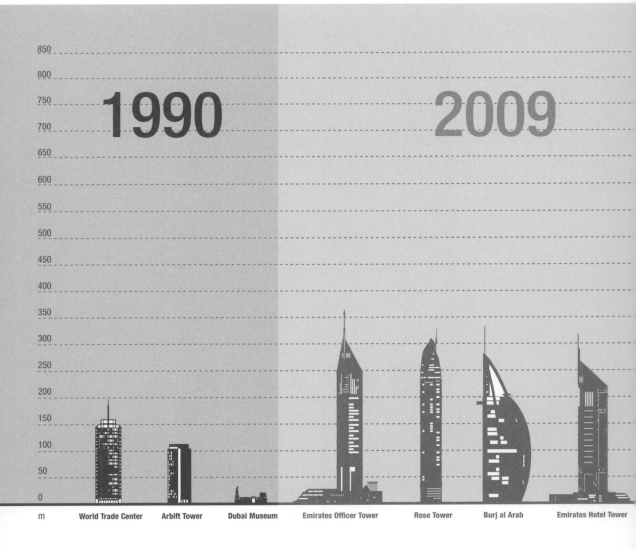

850
800
750

1990

2009

700
650
600
550
500
450
400
350
300
250
200
150
100
50
0

m   **World Trade Center**   **Arbift Tower**   **Dubai Museum**   **Emirates Officer Tower**   **Rose Tower**   **Burj al Arab**   **Emirates Hotel Tower**

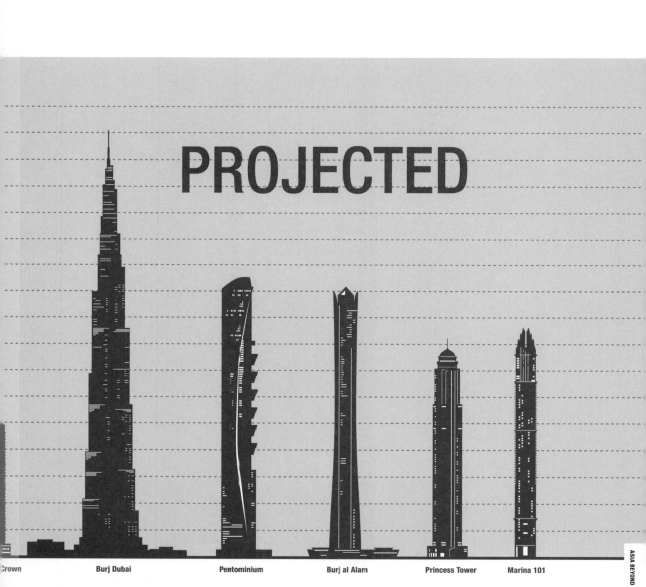

PROJECTED

Crown   Burj Dubai   Pentominium   Burj al Alam   Princess Tower   Marina 101

The government of Dubai predicts that by 2015, it will govern 512 square kilometers of developed area, up from 212 square kilometers in 1993. Dubai is not alone in this kind of growth; six of the ten fastest growing cities in the world are in the East.

OF DUBAI

SHANGHAI

TODAY

10 YEARS AGO

IN THE LAST TEN YEARS, SHANGHAI'S POPULATION INCREASED BY 15%, YET ITS LAND AREA HAS ALMOST DOUBLED.

MUMBAI

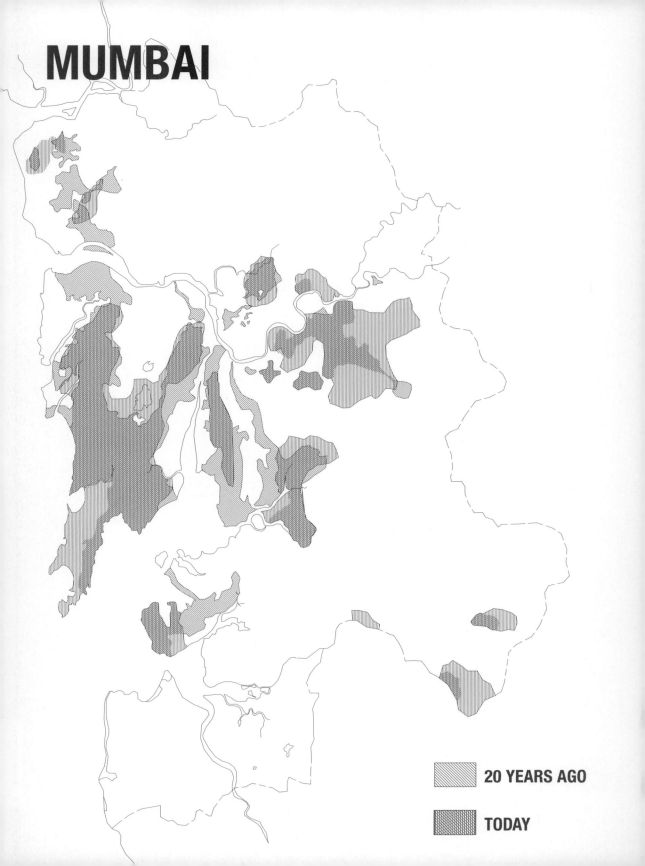

20 YEARS AGO

TODAY

MUMBAI'S BUILT-UP AREA HAS INCREASED BY 60% IN THE PAST 20 YEARS, MEASURING NOW ALMOST 1,000 SQUARE KILOMETERS.

IF IT EXHIBITED THE DENSITY OF A TYPICAL AMERICAN CITY, MUMBAI WOULD BE 15 TIMES ITS CURRENT SIZE.

DUBAI

DUBAI IN 1990

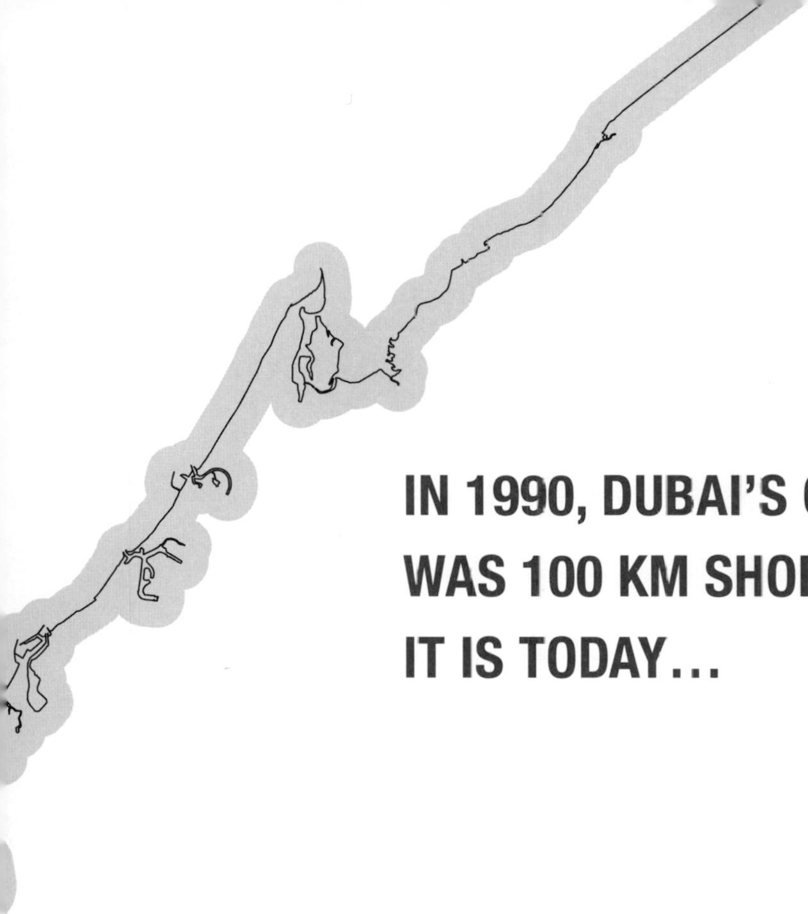

IN 1990, DUBAI'S COASTLINE
WAS 100 KM SHORTER THAN
IT IS TODAY…

DUBAI

DUBAI TODAY

...BECAUSE TODAY, IT INCLUDES THREE PALMS (ONE UNDER CONSTRUCTION), ONE WORLD, AND A PEARL.

PLACED IDENTITIES: TALES FROM THE -AI CITIES

BY PHILIP SCHMUNK WITH YIWEN ZHU

Rapid urbanization and soaring economic growth in major Asian cities has brought about a condition where enormous areas of land are being developed at once. Throughout Asia projects are being built at the outer edge of cities as large territories open for development as a result of new infrastructure or government policies promising grand opportunities within short timeframes. These developments are often the scale of new towns, requiring comprehensive planning and amenities, but lacking the cultural or historical background that might lend the place a distinct identity.

The scale and development speed of new towns often result in places lacking a human scale or familiarity. Nearly instant developments lack the local character that develops incrementally over time based on habits and inclinations of occupants in more traditional neighborhoods.

In Asia a number of shortcuts are used to establish a unique place identity. Although China, India, and the United Arab Emirates share the basic condition of unprecedented urban growth, a number of different strategies for developing identity in new towns have arisen in each context.

SHANGHAI

Abstraction of urban principles can introduce new development models to a foreign context.

In Shanghai the urban core is already densely developed and government has adopted policies aimed at shifting development pressures away from the center, transitioning the city to a poly-centric growth model. The 2001 "One City, Nine Towns" regional planning system introduced a strategy of developing new towns each related to a industry development sector around the core city. Wishing to avoid a "thousand towns sharing the same face" -type monochromatic development seen elsewhere in China, each of the nine towns was to follow a different international style.

The idea of international style was interpreted differently in each of the New Towns. In cases such as the English "Thames Town", a transferred style is instantly recognizable, with statues of Shakespeare and Churchill and a number of English buildings copied directly down to the lettering on windows. Other interpretations of foreign style have been more nuanced. Citta di Pujiang, the Italian new town in Pudong, is unlike what you might expect. The development has no Corinthian or Ionic columns and no Baroque fountains. Instead, the Italian design firm Gregotti Associati adapted deeper ideas about the structure of the Italian city into the design. While architects may think of Giuseppe Terragni's work in Como, the result is a project does not jump out as blatantly Italian to the casual observer. Instead a consistent order and scale pervades the project from city block to housing interior. This abstraction appears to help the translation to a Chinese context, which can recognize some of the same basic elements in the Chinese city. One of Pujiang's great successes has been the implementation of a mixed pattern of housing and urbanization into Shanghai along with international standards of quality and construction.

DIVERSE APPROACHES FOR ESTABLISHING IDENTITY IN LARGE SCALE DEVELOPMENTS HAVE EMERGED AS ASIAN CITIES CONFRONT GROWTH.

While many urban developments in China today are criticized either for lacking a clear style or containing an overwhelming mixture of different styles, the hope is that Shanghai's nine new towns will introduce a number of strategies into the market during this period of opportunity and open the future direction of the city.

MUMBAI

A response and reaction to existing conditions can form the basis of a new identity.

In India, a government agenda of socioeconomic distribution led to the planning of a "twin city" for Mumbai. Navi Mumbai was designed to support a better quality of life than what was available across the Thane Creek in increasing congested Mumbai, especially for middle and lower classes. The expanding layers of the city had further removed the urban poor from opportunities. Navi Mumbai was intended as a solution to the challenges in Mumbai and would integrate socioeconomic groups in a diversified setting, avoid ethnic enclaves and reducing social inequalities.

Although Navi Mumbai was planned as a "twin city" to Mumbai, the relationship is actually more like a counterbalance. The identity of Navi Mumbai is defined by with respect to the original city. Where Mumbai is congested, Navi Mumbai is open. Where Mumbai has difficulty housing the urban poor, Navi Mumbai is a city with multiple employment centers and a without slums.

The completion of the Vashi Bridge across Thane creek in the 1970's connected the Mumbai Peninsula directly to the mainland and opened a large area of land for development. By some accounts, the project is the largest new town anywhere with 14 nodes intended to accommodate 100,000 people apiece. Here the town grows sector by sector. Nodes are made up of 20 - 40 sectors, which each are self sustainable. Navi Mumbai follows a pattern of planning similar to that set out by Le Corbusier in his vision for Chandigarh. Each Sector has a comprehensive group of amenities such as schools and medical facilities. This process of growth creates a more even urban fabric than what exists in Mumbai.

DUBAI

Replication of familiar forms can trigger place associations and fantasy. The growth of Dubai has become increasingly interesting as developments expand from the coast outward over the water and inward over the sandy dunes.

One of Dubai's many iconic projects underway is Falconcity of Wonders. The project constructs identity through the use of instantly recognizable forms such as the Eiffel Tower, the Great Pyramids, etc. The name, Falconcity of Wonders, means quite literally that the great wonders of the world are recreated here and that the plan is in the shape of a giant falcon. The project copies from around the world to produce a fantasy environment. The fantasy of visiting the great landmarks of the world in a single journey becomes itself an attraction. Dubai follows the formula of replication which has succeeded in Las Vegas and Disneyland for decades. While this strategy has been used to entertain and delight visitors in other locations, at Falconcity familiar forms support a resident population and the displacement of these forms from their cultural context is taken as an opportunity to reconsider their use. Here, the Pyramids of Giza are transformed from tombs of Pharaohs to accommodate residential flats and office space and the Eiffel Tower is adapted for luxury apartments and retail outlets.

The forms used to lend Falconcity of Wonders its identity may be its biggest challenge. The flacon shape of the plan leaves little room for flexibility or growth and the main structures cannot be adapted or added to without discarding their image. The images of Falconcity also mark places in history. By looking back to other times and locations, Falconcity has missed the opportunity to create something original for Dubai. Looking back has made it difficult to look forward.

THE ROLE OF IDENTITY WILL CONTINUE TO EVOLVE AS GROWTH IN ASIA CONTINUES. AT THE MOMENT IDENTITY SERVES TO DIFFERENTIATE NEW PROJECTS AS THEY COMPETE IN A BROAD FIELD OF DEVELOPMENT.

The success of these approaches to identity will best be understood after a period of time and use. The initial character of the new towns will certainly change as communities inhabit the space and develop social patterns unique to that place. Identity presented at the outset serves as a placeholder until more authentic locally formed characteristics take hold. This is already happening in Shanghai and Navi Mumbai, but may prove more difficult in Dubai, where identity is so blatant. In this last case, locally formed identity will likely exist alongside the legacy of the initial concept rather than replace it.

Identity helps to define and locates a place in a larger context of globalization. Scales and speed of development tend toward replication of elements, but maybe that's not as great of a problem as it seems. With the increasing mobility and ability to communicate easily, identity derived from our physical context may lose importance, and maybe that's alright.

Towering Ambitions in the Emirates. Fifteen years ago, there were just a small handful of skyscrapers in the gulf city-states such as Dubai, Abu Dhabi, Doha and Bahrain. Today, there are hundreds.

Echoing the migrations of the American sun belt, there are four times as many people living in the United Arab Emirates and twice as many in Bahrain today than there were twenty years ago. Most of them are foreign born.

Towering Ambitions in Beijing. Fifteen years ago, there was one skyscraper taller than 100 meters in Beijing. Today, there are 23.

The building spree in Beijing has attracted the world's top design talent. Five Pritzker Laureates have on projects in the Chinese capital; and the largest architecture firms from the US, the UK and Australia all have offices in the city.

Beijing's Central Business District, which lies 6 kilometers east of the Forbidden City, is a focus for the city's efforts to transform itself. Home to Rem Koolhaas CCTV headquarters, SOM's China World Trade Center and KPF's China Central Place, it didn't exist in 1990.

Today there are more than two million square meters of office space in Beijing's relatively small Central Business District. In 2004, there were just over 700,000, in the entire city.

徐工集团

OMOGENIZATION

The renderer has taken on an important new role in the Asian cityscape, as messenger of an idealized future.

In bold billboards, civic authorities tout visions of clinical spotlessness, a far cry from the hot and sweaty color of the traditional Asian city.

机场大道

Where am I?

a) Irvine
b) Bangalore
c) Jacksonville, FL
d) Hangzhou

Where am I?

a) Beijing
b) Seoul
c) Kuala Lumpur
d) Guangzhou

Where am I?

a) Singapore
b) Kuala Lumpur
c) Manila
d) Taipei

Where am I?

a) Taiyuan
b) Shijiazguang
c) Lanzhou
d) Datong

Where am I?

a) Glendale, CA
b) Manila
c) Wollongong, NSW
d) Bethesda, MD

Where am I?

a) Mumbai
b) Lahore
c) Dubai
d) Doha

Where am I?

a) Venice
b) Las Vegas
c) Macau
d) All of the above

BEYOND HOMOGENIZATION: IN CHINA, A NEW REGIONALISM IN PUBLIC SPACE

Much has been written recently about the transformation of China's cities. Especially with its ambitious Olympic Games, the signature architectural commissions in Beijing such as the National Stadium, the Aquatic Center and the CCTV Headquarters have all been the subject of ample critical ilk. At the same time, the underbelly of China's relentless development is now a frequent storyline: anonymous cities, smoggy skies, dirty water. It is a theme that is touched upon in this book itself.

But far from the centers of fashion, in cities such as Bengbu, Kunshan and Taiyuan – places largely unfamiliar to those outside China – we have recently completed three public domain projects that quietly point a new way forward for emerging Chinese cities. In each case, the local government turned to us to develop a new contribution to the public realm to address the ecological and physical scars of the economic revolution in their midst. In a progressive and contemporary way, each design carries forward the world's oldest land design tradition, that of the Chinese. They use local materials, hardscapes, planting, hues and references, but they are also characteristically Modern. For the first time in recent history, there is a beautiful, shared domain in each place.

What is remarkable about these works is their location: not Beijing, not Shanghai, in fact quite the opposite. There is Taiyuan, one of the most polluted cities on Earth, in the heart of China's coal belt; there is Bengbu, home to hundreds of food processing plants, and there is Kunshan, home to many Taiwanese-owned factories. These three projects build on a portfolio of public realm in secondary cities like Wuxi, Tianjin and Suzhou. This new body of work is in far-out locales, not where one would expect to find the best in new public space in China. For a country with dozens of mega-cities, and literally hundreds that would qualify anywhere else as 'major,' it is a promising way forward.

CELEBRATING LOCAL QUALITIES

Bengbu, a city of 600,000, commissioned us in 2005 to master plan a forty square kilometer area surrounding its neighbor, Dragon Lake, in an effort to lend an attractive new face for the entire city. The initiative provided an excellent opportunity to reorient Bengbu, shaping its future urban expansion in a way that will respect the natural assets of Dragon Lake. As the first phase of the master plan's public space implementation, the Bridge Park is a signature parkland that is aesthetically pleasing, environmentally friendly and culturally relevant.

Completed in early 2008, the park's design emphasizes Bengbu itself, in order to impart a distinct identity on both the city and the lake.

LI LAKE PARK, WUXI

DRAGON LAKE BRIDGE PARK, BENGBU

Locally appropriate plant species that fit the climate and soils of Bengbu provide a welcoming habitat for local birds, fish and insects. For people, shared spaces come alive and take on new meaning in the use of local methods and materials in the design of promenades, pavilions and bridges, which dot the landscape. Environmental sensitivity was integral to the design process and is evident in the minimal use of earth-work to preserve original land forms, the utilization of low-impact design to reduce and filter storm-water runoff entering Dragon Lake.

Fundamentally what the park does is help this third tier city revitalize its competitive position and quality of life. It shows how land design can be used to alter a city's identity for the better. The park links Bengbu to Dragon Lake, creating the city's first shared space that fosters interaction among people, and with nature. And it is just the beginning of what is in store for this growing city – the Bridge Park is the first of several pieces of a broader master plan, the rest of which are now being detailed.

BEYOND INDUSTRY, A CITY OF AMENITIES

While Kunshan may seem a diminutive satellite of its neighbors Shanghai and Suzhou, it is no small place. More than one million people call this burgeoning city home, and typical of many cities in China's Yangtze River Delta,

it is a manufacturing hub. Perhaps its most famous export is the iPod as thousands are made here and then sent to all four corners of the world. The local government approached us to design an exciting new park that would revitalize the old city core and would also communicate its economic success. The response, which opened in 2008, is a blend of urban design, architecture and landscape ingenuity that incorporates existing economic and recreational programs, improves water quality and enhances the site's human scale.

Kunshan's Civic Plaza is an active place that encourages human activity, from sport to culture. The designers used existing topography to create an amphitheatre, retrofitted an existing athletic field, while incorporating new architectural furnishings such as raised walkways, media walls projecting historical and cultural information, and performance and seating areas that are embedded into the topography. The park, which hugs a river, was also an opportunity to clean up the water with a new wetland waterfront and lily pond that act as natural treatment systems.

The complexity of the urban site enabled the design to become a truly multidisciplinary project that morphs architecture and

DRAGON LAKE BRIDGE PARK, BENGBU

KUNSHAN CIVIC PLAZA

landscape, and celebrates the city's history and contemporary prosperity. A deep connection is made with Kunshan's waterside, blurring the boundaries between built and natural zones, encouraging residents to experience the delicacies of their local landscape. Today, the Civic Plaza is full of activity. Elderly residents wake up and perform Tai Chi on the riverfront terraces, while during the day young athletes playing football on the field, and by evening, lovers can be seen meandering through the poetic web of walkways.

HERITAGE COMES BACK ALIVE

Taiyuan is emblematic of much of what has happened to the contemporary Chinese cityscape. An ancient city with an important place in Chinese history, the city has lost much of its unique character and architectural heritage. Its location in the heart of China's coal belt has also made its air quality among the worst in the world. It is in this context that the city of Taiyuan has tasked us to redevelop the city's public spaces. This streetscape is the first of several ongoing projects that aim to raise the quality and tenor of Taiyuan's urban environment.

The Yingze Boulevard is the main artery in the heart of this teaming city of 3.4 million people, and is framed by government and commercial buildings. The overall atmosphere was lacking in architectural character. It could be anywhere in China, and certainly did not feel like the heart of a city with more than two millennia of history. It was this concern for loss of heritage that drove the overhaul of this civic corridor. The key elements to the streetscape improvement along the Boulevard's center-city 2.5 kilometers stretch were the design of various sculptural and lighting features. They range from the striking and contemporary (17-meter pole lights that act as a canopy to the traffic below) to the subtle and traditional (luminous bollard features clad in traditional patterns that evoke the colors of the vernacular cityscape). Mature trees were preserved and new lighting screens create a gentle buffer between vehicle and pedestrian traffic. These features are intended to draw attention away from the area's drab architecture by restoring a sense of distinctiveness to this historic promenade.

Most of all, the design is about heritage – reviving traditional aesthetics in various pieces of the streetscape. In invoking local patterns and colors in such a way, Taiyuan is quietly becoming Taiyuan again.

NATURE AND CITY

In the heart of the Yangtze River Delta – a hotbed of people lush with productivity – is the city of Wuxi. Like Kunshan, Wuxi

YINGZE BOULEVARD, TAIYUAN

is nestled between Suzhou and giant Shanghai and by the early 2000s had come to be dominated by industry in a very profound way. As many cities in China's vast mid-section, Wuxi began as a lakefront settlement. And like many of these cities in recent times, the connection between lake and town has been broken.

We have assisted the local government in correcting that link, developing large waterfront parklands that front both city and lake. With an appropriate balance of naturalism and deliberative open space design over 220 hectares of once decrepit landfill, new community attractions and amenities have been introduced for the first time. Eschewing hierarchy for fusion, the design fuses art with lighting, landmarks with structures. At various edges of the water, a mix of traditionally-inspired contemporary pavilions reintroduce the ritualism of meandering through a garden space typical of the Chinese landscape.

Ambitious and progressive, the local authorities were eager for a multi-layered approach that moved beyond landscape architecture itself by integrating regional planning, environmental quality concerns and the long-term identity of the city. The early success of the parklands has provided a set of 'green lungs' for an otherwise polluted city, and has advanced ecology into the consciousness of local residents and visitors alike.

BRINGING PEOPLE BACK OUTSIDE

For centuries, the Hai River has played a central role in Tianjin, a port city of 10 million about an hour's train ride from Beijing. In Chinese, the city's name refers to the river's relationship with Ming Dynasty Emperors; it also was the backdrop for Tianjin's colonial concessions. After asking us to plan the clean-up and regeneration of an 18 kilometer stretch of the river bank, the municipality turned to us design a five kilometer stretch of the embankment promenade.

The embankment's intersection with river and city was drab and negleced. In many ways, it did not even exist. Instead, there was nothing between the river and the city, there was a gaping hole, a vortex into which local character and quality of life fell.

In crafting an embankment, the designers looked to culture – not just to vernacular colors and symbolism, but to habits, which is why today on the Hai River Embankment, at the very heart of a city of ten million people, people are dancing, practicing tai chi, fishing, picnicking, bicycling, diving into the water. This is all possible because of a tapestry of open spaces, squares, plazas

HAI RIVER EMBANKMENT, TIANJIN

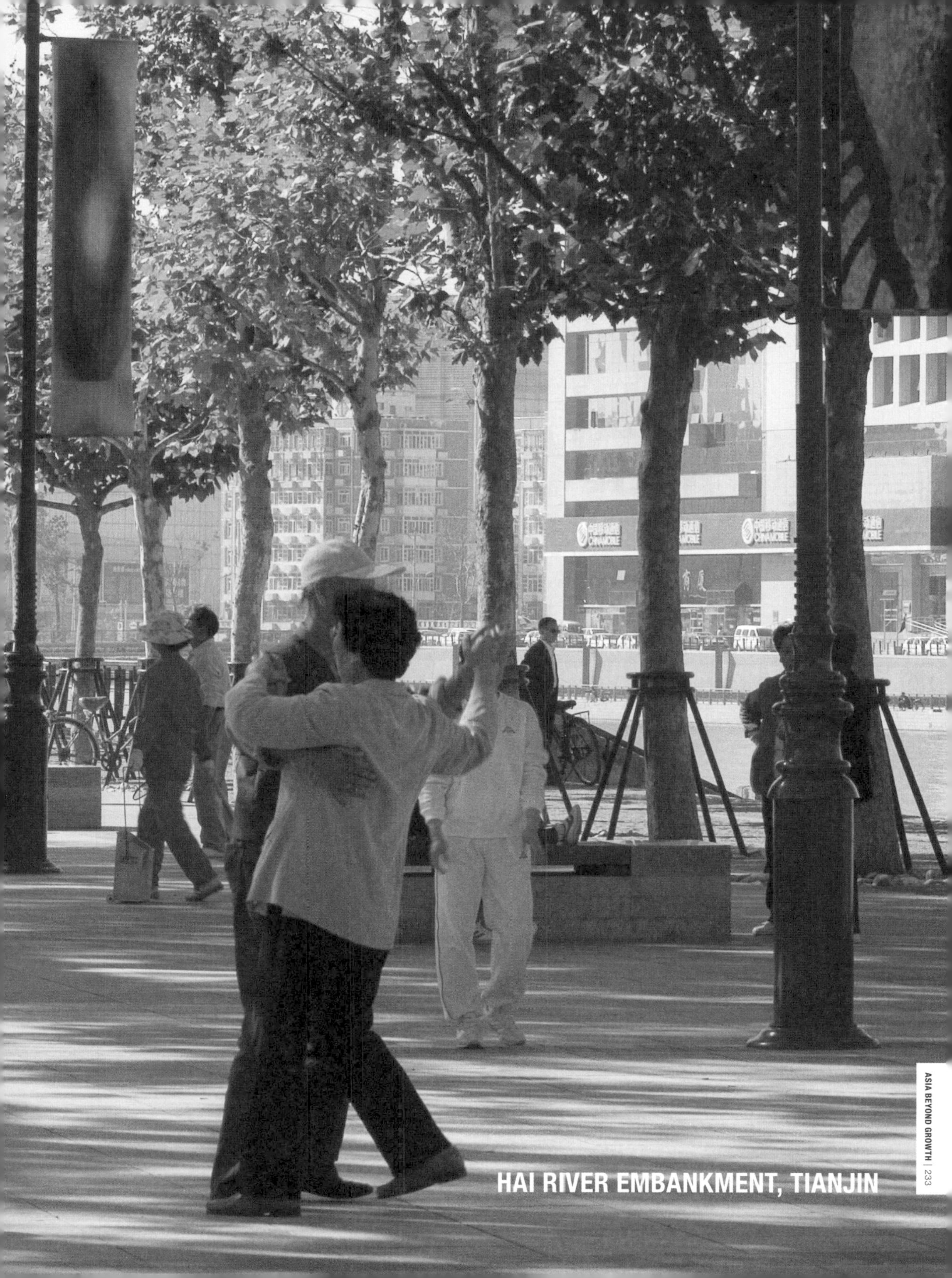

HAI RIVER EMBANKMENT, TIANJIN

JINJI LAKE, SUZHOU

and promenades that together unify into a great embankment. All actively engage with the water and are dotted with a series of sculptural lights and bollards that provide an accord to the embankment and those who use it, echoing the best in waterfront design worldwide. It is a cosmopolitan statement for the locals.

RESTORING A TRADITION

If any city has a greater hold on the imagination of Chinese lore, it is Suzhou. Graced with ancient gardens and home to much of the country's literary past, the city of Suzhou was immortalized centuries ago – an Eastern foil to Marco Polo's Venice – replete with the canals, the distinct architecture and the splendor of renaissance. Most valuable though is Suzhou's legacy of landscape. The old city is dotted with dozens of priceless gardens that constitute an important part of humanity's tangible heritage.

Looking to the future, the central government had designated a new area adjacent to the historic core that would usher in a new kind of renaissance. Just like old Suzhou itself, it would need gardens equal to the task. Centered around Jinji Lake, we were brought in to plan and design 550 hectares of open space that would be a focus for the city's future, and in the process has written the newest chapter in the evolving story of the Chinese landscape tradition.

Divided into five districts, the Jinji Lake open space system brings together local character, spatial organization and people-friendly places. These occur in a harbor-side plaza, an elegant waterfront promenade, a grand cultural corridor, a meandering camphor and maple forest, and an aspirational Millennium Plaza. Emphatically contemporary in both concept and form, the Jinji parks though provide an apt complement to old Suzhou's legendary ancient gardens. In a sense, just as the old gardens did, they portend a new time of glory for an ancient city.

In Suzhou and these five other cities across China, public space is coming back alive in a way that slowly begins to allude to a future that may yet restore character and uniqueness of place to the Chinese city. What is dramatic about these public spaces (and the more that are coming down the pipeline) is that this is all occurring in a context hat just three short decades befcre was in the throws of the brutally insane cultural revolution. We work with these cities is a story of firsts – the first park, the first place for public gathering, the first time any nvestment has been made in restoring a sense of heritage for decades. Far from the eyes of Beijing and Shanghai, these cities are quietly looking beyond growth.

JINJI LAKE, SUZHOU

JINJI LAKE, SUZHOU

LI LAKE PARK, WU XI

LI LAKE PARK, WU XI

HAI RIVER EMBANKMENT, TIANJIN

HAI RIVER EMBANKMENT, TIANJIN

KUNSHAN CIVIC PLAZA

YINGZE BOULEVARD, TAIYUAN

DRAGON LAKE BRIDGE PARK, BENGBU

IFRAVESTMENT

Massive investment in new infrastructure across Asia's emerging cities is raising the bar worldwide in the quality of shared public goods such as airports, public transport, and exhibition facilities.

SHANGHAI

 **390km**

Total length of overland roads in 1997

 **944km**

Total length in 2006

 **6,264**

Number of buses in 1997

Number in 2006

 **96**

Number of municipal trains in 1997

Number in 2006

= 50km

= 1,000

= 100

17,284

829

SHANGHAI

 **111**

Number of ferries in 1997

 **53**

Number in 2006

 **11,298**

Number of taxis in 1997

Number in 2006

0km

Municipal rail line length in 1990

 **125km**

Length in 2004

🚕 **48,022**

MUMBAI

 6

Number of airport projects since 1990

New railroads since then...

9

...and new roads,

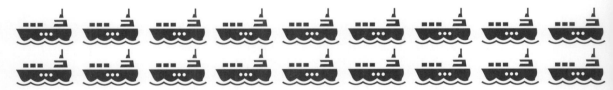

and new seaport developments.

Total road length in 2006

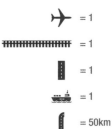

= 1

= 1

= 1

= 1

= 50km

19

1,898km

DUBAI

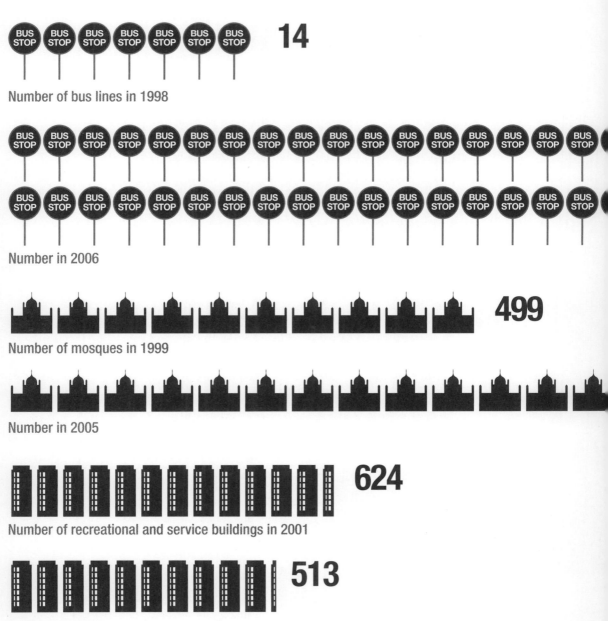

14

Number of bus lines in 1998

Number in 2006

499

Number of mosques in 1999

Number in 2005

624

Number of recreational and service buildings in 2001

513

Number in 2006

= 2

= 50

= 50

88

890

Asia is home to five of the world's ten busiest airports, its four best airports, anc its (current and future) largest airports.

Increase in air passenger traffic

	152%	447%	353%	309%
	1998 - 2005	1998 - 2005	1998 - 2007	1998 - 2007
	HKG	**DOH**	**DXB**	**PEK**
	Hong Kong International Airport	Doha International Airport	Dubai International Airport	Beijing International Airport

Airport Traffic

Top 10
World Airports

INTERNATIONAL
PASSENGERS 2007

01	London (LHR)	61,348,340
02	Paris	51,888,936
03	Amsterdam	45,940,939
04	Frankfurt	45,697,176
05	Hong kong	43,274,765
06	Tokyo	33,860,094
07	Singapore	33,368,099
08	London (LGW)	30,016,837
09	Bangkok	29,587,773
10	Dubai	27,925,522

CARGO
(METRIC TONNES in 2007)

01	Memphis	3,392,081
02	Hong Kong	3,609,780
03	Anchorage	2,691,395
04	Seoul	2,336,572
05	Tokyo	2,280,830
06	Shanghai	2,168,122
07	Paris	2,130,724
08	Frankfurt	2,127,646
09	Louisville	1,983,032
10	Singapore	1,931,881

INTERNATIONAL
FREIGHT
(METRIC TONNES in 2007)

01	Hong Kong	3,578,991
02	Seoul	2,307,817
03	Tokyo	2,235,548
04	Anchorage	2,129,796
05	Frankfurt	1,996,632
06	Singapore	1,911,214
07	Paris	1,832,283
08	Shanghai	1,829,041
09	Taipei	1,686,423
10	Amsterdam	1,152,504

IMPORTING

ARCHITECTURE

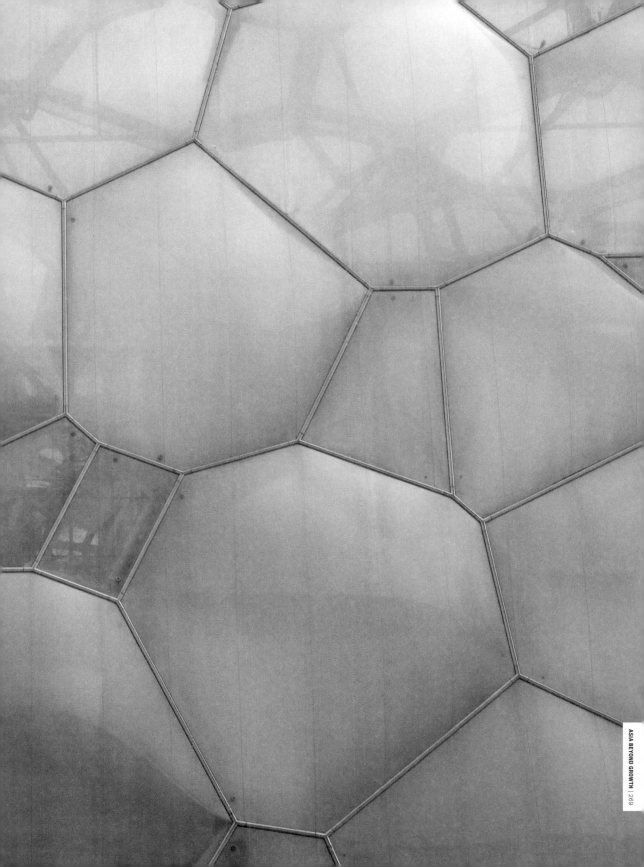

In 1997, we had zero Design + Planning employees stationed in Asia. Today, there are more than 400 in six studios.

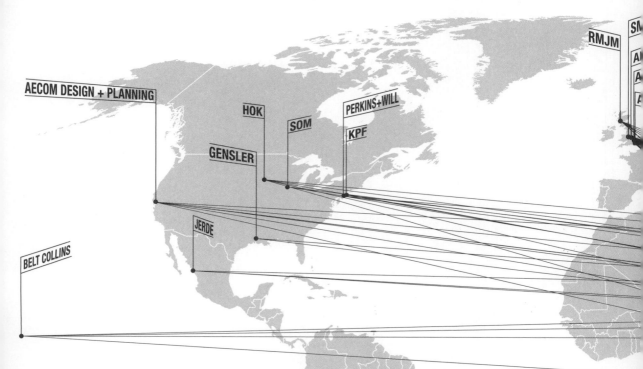

AECOM DESIGN + PLANNING

HOK

SOM

PERKINS+WILL

KPF

GENSLER

RMJM

SM

JERDE

BELT COLLINS

WESTERN FIRMS, ASIAN STUDIOS

WOODS BAGOT

PTW

HASSELL

The largest buildings for three Pritzker laureates – Rem Koolhaas, Lord Foster, and Herzog & de Meuron – are all located in Beijing.

供电公司

电站工程

中 国 建 筑

H-project
Seoul, Korea
1995

New Seoul International Airport
Seoul, Korea
1995

Electronic Showroom
Seoul, Korea
1996

Togok Towers
Seoul, Korea
1996

Hyperbuilding
Bangkok, Thailand
1997

Hanoi New Town Masterplan
Hanoi, Vietnam
1997

Inchon-Song Do New Town
Inchon, Korea
1998

CCTV - Television Cultural Centre
Beijing, China
2002

CCTV - TV station and headquarters
Beijing, China
2002

Guangzhou Opera House
Guangzhou, China
2002

CCTV Media Park
Beijing, China
2002

CCTV Service Building
Beijing, China
2002

Beijing Central Business District
Beijing, China
2003

Beijing Preservation
Beijing, China
2003

Beijing Books Building
Beijing, China
2003

Multi Media Building
Hong Kong
2004

Penang Tropical City
Penang, Malaysia
2004

S-Project
Seoul, Korea
2004

Prada Shanghai
Shanghai, China
2004

China National Museum
Beijing, China
2004

Shanghai Expo 2010
Shanghai, China
2004

Prada Skirt
Shanghai, China
2004

Leeum Museum
Seoul, Korea
2004

Jeddah International Airport
Jeddah, Saudi Arabia
2005

SNU Museum of Art
Seoul, Korea
2005

Porche Towers
Dubai, UAE
2006

Shenzhen Stock Exchange
Shenzhen, China
2006

Qatar Education City - 3 Buildings
Doha, Qatar
2006

Rak Jebel Al Jais Mountain Resort
Ras Al Khaimah, UAE
2006

Dubai Renaissance
Dubai, UAE
2006

Rak Convention & Exhibition Centre
Ras Al Kaimah, UAE
2006

Rak Gateway
Ras Al Khaimah, UAE
2006

Scotts Tower
Singapore
2006

Kuwai Al-Rai Masterplan
Kuwait City, Kuwait
2006

Rak Structure Plan
Ras Al Khaimah, UAE
2007

Amaty Science Campus
Almaty, Kazakhstan
2007

Waterfront City
Dubai, UAE
2008

The Peak
Hong Kong
1982 - 1983

Guggenheim Museum
Talchung, Taiwan

Abu Dhabi Bridge
Abu Dhabi, UAE
1997

Soho City
Beijing, China

Doha Tower
Doha, Quatar

One North Singapore Masterplan
Singapore
2001

Performance Arts Centre
Abu Dhabi, UAE
2007

Guangzhou Opera House
Guangzhou, China
2007

Dancing Towers
Dubai, UAE
2007

Dubai Opera House
Dubai, UAE
2007

HSBC Headquarters
Hong Kong
1986

Chep Lap Kok Airport
Hong Kong
1998

Expo Station
Singapore
2000

HACTL Superterminal
Hong Kong
1998

Jiushi Corportation Headquarters
Shanghai, China
2001

Pertonas University of Technology
Seri Iskandar, Malaysia
2004

Alder Central Market
Abu Dhabi, UAE

Beach Road
Singapore
2007

Beijing Airport
Beijing, China
2008

Central Markets
Astana, Kazakhstan
2003

Khan Shatyry Entertainment Centre
Astana, Kazakhstan
2008

Masdar Development
Abu Dhabi, UAE
2007

Palace of Peace and Reconciliation
Astana, Kazakhstan
2006

Shanghai Expo Theme Pavillion
Shanghai, China
2010

Supreme Court
Singapore
2005

The Index
Dubai, UAE

West Kowloon Cultural District
Hong Kong
2002

The Troika
Kuala Lumpur, Malaysia
2009

The Blue City Oman
Muscat, Oman
2008

Doha Airport
Doha, Qatar
1976

New Airport of Jakarta
Jakarta, Indonesia
1991

Brunel Airport
Brunel
1987

Kuala Lumpur Airport
Kuala Lumpur, Malaysia
1984

Dong Muang Airport
Bangkok, Thailand
1985

Manilla Airport
Manilla, Phillippines
1999

Airport of Sanya
Hainan Island, China
1994

Borobudur Hotel
Jakarta, Indonesia
1991

New Seoul Metropolitan Airport
Seoul, Korea
1992

Doha Airport
Doha, Qatar
1993

Bangkok Airport
Bangckk, Thailand
1994

Shanghai Pudong International Airport
Shanghai, China
1999

Abu Dhabi Airport Terminal 2
Abu Dhabi, UAE
2005

Shanghai Industrial Museum
Shanghai, China
1997

Guangzhou Gymnasium
Guangzhou, China
2001

Guangzhou Daily Cultural Plaza
Guangzhou, China
1998

Guangzhou Baiyun Airport
Guangzhou, China
1998

Ningbo Airport - New Terminal
Dongshe
Ningbo, China
1998

National Grand Theatre of China
Beijing, China
2005

Dubai Airport
Dubai, UAE
2005

Oriental Arts Centre
Shanghai, China
2004

Guangdong Science Centre
Guangzhou, China
2003

Beijing Business District Core
Beijing, China
2003

Shanghai Diamond Site
Shanghai, China
2003

Suzhou Science and Cultural Art Centre
Suzhou, China
2003

Beijing World Forum Village
Beijing, China
2003

Technology and Science Enterpising
Centre
Chengdu, China
2006

France Ambassy in Beijing
Beijing, China
2004

Hotel for Shanghai Oriental Art Centre
Shanghai, China
2007

Guangzhou New Library
Guangzhou, China
2005

Hotel in Macau
Macau
2005

Oceanus Complex in Macau
Macau
2007

Chengdu Court House
Chengdu, China
2005

← OMA unbuilt

← OMA built

← ZAHA HADID ARCHITECTS unbuilt

← ZAHA HADID ARCHITECTS built

← FOSTER + PARTNERS unbuilt

← FOSTER + PARTNERS built

← PAUL ANDREU ARCHITECTS unbuilt

← PAUL ANDREU ARCHITECTS built

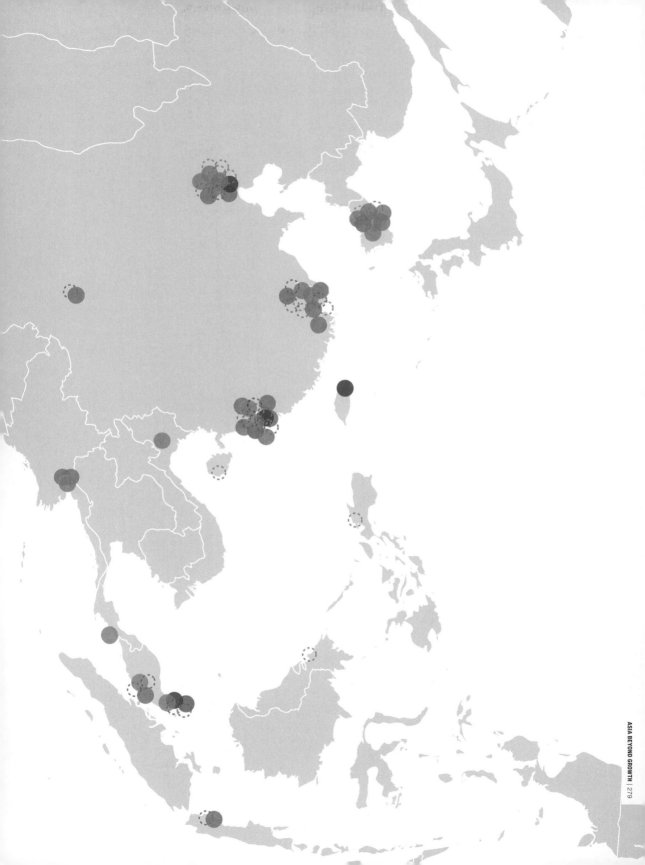

HANGZHOU, CHINA

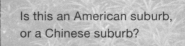
Is this an American suburb,
or a Chinese suburb?

Is this German Gothic or Emirati retail?

DUBAI, UAE

Milanese Galleria...in the desert.

DUBAI, UAE

MUMBAI, INDIA

Baroque Cupolas and Neo-Classical Victory...in India.

LEARNING FROM MACAU: THE HERITAGE STRIP

WITH CHENG SZE HON AND NANORI MATSUDA, THE UNIVERSITY OF HONG KONG

Intimacy and heritage are inexorably linked. Old cities are often compact ones full of small houses, pocket parks, narrow alleyways and neighborhood piazzas. It is smallness that often characterizes historic city fabric. In the context of fast-paced growth, it is this elusive smallness that is often overlooked and destroyed, usually in favor of something larger. In Macau, smallness has for centuries been part of the city's character even as much of its contemporary growth has focused on large-scale casinos and hotel developments.

In the midst of the Cotai Strip, there is a lesser known Heritage Strip – a corridor of cityscape that not only lends Macau much of its gravitas and local sense of self, but can also be a focus for future enjoyment by both visitors and residents alike. This Strip has been delineated in the work of Sze Hon, a student of architecture at the University of Hong Kong under the guidance of Professor Nanori Matsuda.

Macau was settled in the 1500s by the Portuguese, and remained a Portuguese holding until 1999. The city-state has been an important gateway through which European culture, traditions and lifestyles entered China. This duality of culture continues today and is firmly evident in the textures of the city, in its history and administration, as well as physical features such as its architecture, gardens and public spaces. What stands in much of old Macau today resembles the ambling Mediterranean character of a Portuguese town, built at a sixteenth-century (small) scale.

In 2005, the historic center of Macau was recognized as such with its inscription on UNESCO's World Heritage List. It is hoped that the recognition will help to promote responsible tourism in Macau, raising

IT IS THOUGH MACAU'S VALUABLE HERITAGE SITES AND CONSERVED NEIGHBORHOODS THAT COULD OFFER THE MOST COMPELLING TOURISM EXPERIENCE: A GENUINE URBAN ENVIRONMENT THAT IS ROOTED IN PLACE, ROOTED IN HISTORY AND ROOTED IN CULTURE.

awareness both within the territory and overseas that encourages appreciation of heritage and more importantly provides a positive influence over the future of heritage conservation.

SMALLNESS RETAINS THE SPIRIT OF CULTURE AND HISTORY OF THE PLACE, AND SMALLNESS IN HISTORIC URBAN FABRIC REFLECTS HOW CIVILIZATION CAME TO THIS PLACE, WHAT INFLUENCES LEAD THEM TO CRAFT IT AND HOW THE COMMUNITY DEVELOPED.

Macau's Heritage Strip runs right through the labyrinth of structures that make up its UNESCO World Heritage site. These buildings include the A-ma Temple, the Moorish Barracks, the Mandarin's House, Lilau Square, St. Lawrence's Church, St. Augustine's Square, Senado Square, and the Ruins of St. Paul. Together, they frame a corridor on Macau

Peninsula that can become a new focus for tourism activity, adding an organic dimension to the largely inorganic experience that visiting Macau has become in recent years. Here, the intimacy of old Macau – all plainly there – can become the latest attraction for the new Macau. It provides a focus for unity. Lilau Square is a prime example that shows how smallness is retained. Small white houses along its side streets date from the earliest Portuguese settlements. They frame the square, which hosts three big trees that stand monumentally creating a canopy for local people. The square serves the same function today as it did in centuries past, providing a living and breathing window into uniqueness.

Like Lilau Square, Macau itself is small. It is home to half a million people who are squeezed into an area just under thirty square kilometers. The development coming from tourism and gambling is crowding out the smallness that we find in pockets like Lilau Square. This is exacerbated because Macau itself is small. The development brought on by increases in tourism and gaming business have the potential to crowd out the old. The historic center of Macau is situated in an area of great commercial interest, but one that needs to be properly leveraged by looking to the amenities and features

AN INCREASING NUMBER OF
CONVENTIONS AND INTERNATIONAL
EXPOSITIONS ARE BEING HELD IN
THE NUMEROUS NEW VENUES THAT
DOT THE FRINGE'S OF MACAU'S CITY-
SCAPE. ONE HOUR FROM HONG KONG
BY FERRY, MACAU IS EMERGING AS A
ONE-STOP-FITS-ALL TOURISM
ENVIRONMENT; IF HONG KONG
IS MANHATTAN ON THE
SOUTH CHINA SEA,
THEN

**MACAU IS
ITS VEGAS.**

TOURISM IS MACAU'S FUTURE. MORE VISITORS ARE VISITING THE TERRITORY FOR LEISURE, ENTERTAINMENT AND GAMING, AND ALSO TO EXPLORE THE ANCIENT CITY. IN THE FIRST TEN MONTHS OF 2007, VISITOR ARRIVALS IN MACAU REACHED NEARLY

22 MILLION,

REPRESENTING A

22.6% INCREASE

OVER THE PREVIOUS YEAR.

LIKE COTAI, THE HERITAGE STRIP CAN BE ALIVE, BUT IN A PROFOUNDLY DIFFERENT WAY; ALIVE WITH SUBTLETY, SUGGESTION AND DISCOVERY.

found in the most unlikely of sources – in the programmatic savvy of new land development such as the one in its neighbor to the south, the Cotai Strip.

In order for historic Macau to become a focus for visitors, it needs to groom more secondary elements for tourism accommodation such as food and beverage options, and public toilets. Its narrow streets need to be pedestrianized to push out the vehicular traffic that obstructs human interaction with the space. And as local industry shifts to a business environment dominated by gaming and mega-hotels, local Macanese are moving out of the corridor, abandoning their houses and shops in search of more lucrative opportunities. Tourists are not interested in visiting a dead city.

Assuming the route is pedestrianized, greenery, sitting-out areas, fountains and cafés can be placed alongside, and node points – where

cars, pedestrian, monuments and smallness overlap – can become potential areas for future transformation. Pedestrianization will afford opportunities and new interests for locals and tourists alike, bringing them out into the corridor to walk amidst the heritage. There are three specific locations where smallness could be re-imagined, to create new foci that inject dynamism into the Strip with out overwhelming it. These places are at Lilau Square, St. Lawrence Church and St. Augustine Square. Each of the three carry different implications and offer opportunities for tourists to visit, to experience, and each give clues that guide visitors where to go next.

Node 1 – Lilau Square. The groundwater at Lilau used to be the main source of natural spring water in water, and it is memorialized in a popular Portuguese phrase – "One who drinks from Lilau never forgets Macau." To reflect this compact site's connection to water, a gentle reflecting wall/pool can be incorporated into the Square's architecture. This wall would obscure an existing well, luring visitors to walk around it and discover Lilau's historic place in Macau lore, a place where identity is discovered.

Node 2 – St. Lawrence Church. This church is situated on the southern coastline of the Macau Peninsula, overlooking the sea. Because of its scale, it dominates the surrounding area. It was a significant place for the families of Portuguese sailors in the past, because it is where they would gather to pray and wait for their return from voyages. Tucked at the end of a tiny alleyway off the church is a miniscule Tin-Hau Temple, which served a similar function for Chinese families, but had lived in relative obscurity because of its diminutive size. To gently attract attention to this unknown temple, a simple, contemporary gateway could be built to frame it, within view of St. Lawrence Church. Visually, this would connect the two religious buildings, using its sculptural form to tell a story, and would cue visitors to visit the temple.

Node 3 – St. Augustine Square. The 'patio' is the original term used to describe the early Chinese settlements in Macau. The patio that exists along St. Augustine Square is a new discovery for locals and tourists because it reflects the Chinese architectural elements in contrast with the Portuguese style dominant in and around the Square. A gateway obscures the Ho-Tung Library, a Chinese-style building on the site of the patio, providing a suggestive entry leading visitors to the library and the garden behind.

EACH ELEMENT NOT ONLY REFLECTS THE CONTEXT OF THE AREA, BUT ALSO COLLECTIVELY TELLS A STORY ABOUT THE AREA, ENGAGING VISITORS AND MAKING THE HERITAGE COME ALIVE.

Unlike Cotai, they are simple and small architectural gestures. These are places where space, place and heritage can come together to create a cityscape with the best kind of branding and experiences to lure visitors – those that celebrate what has been here for hundreds of years. More than preserving history, they tell histories.

RISING WEALTH

In 2008, Macau surpassed Las Vegas as the world's gambling capital.

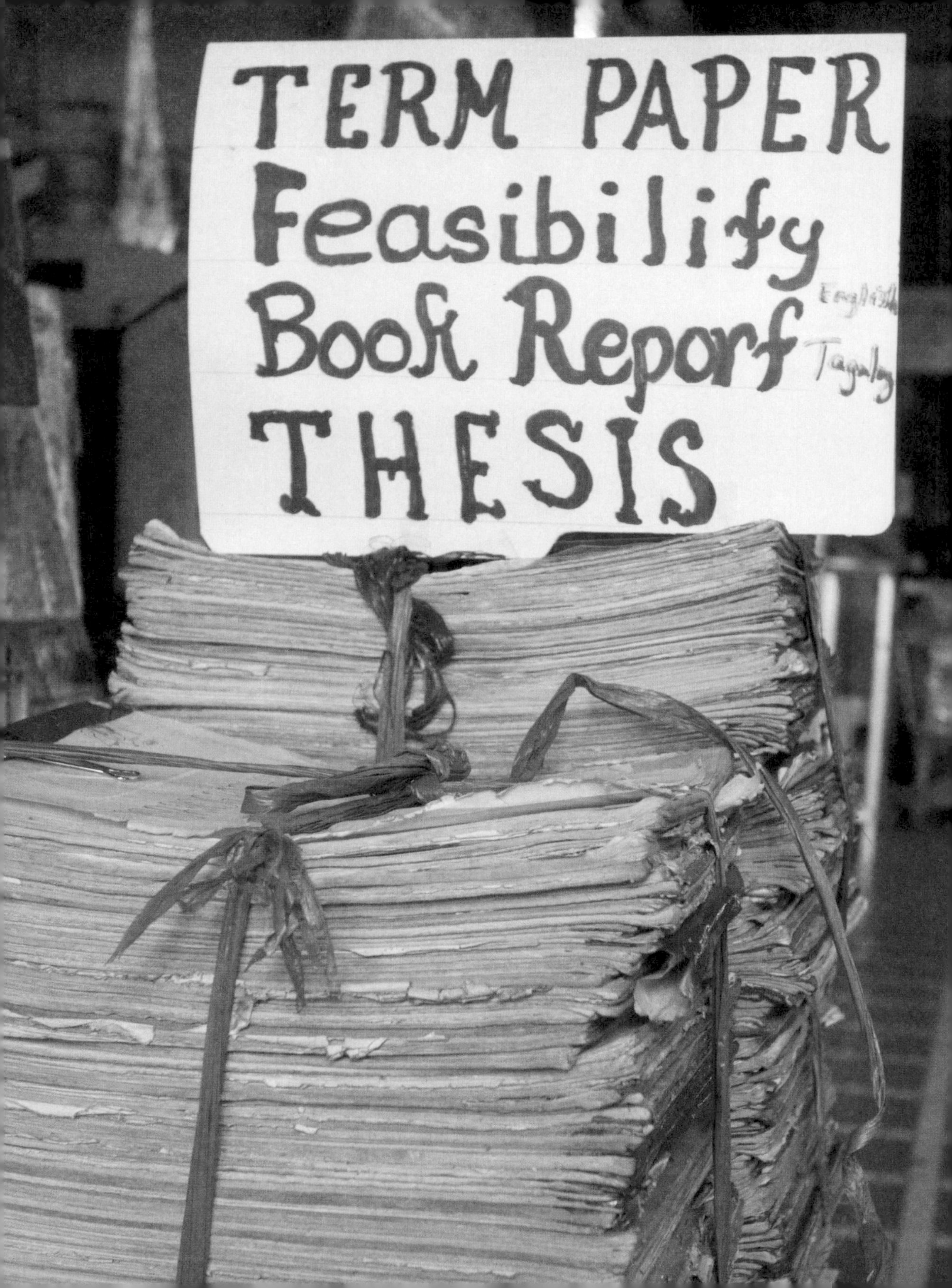
TERM PAPER
Feasibility
Book Report
THESIS
Tagalog

Today, literacy rates and levels of education in emerging societies are at their highest in history.

GROWING
LITERACY

Percentage increase
in the period from 1990-2004.

1+1=

China (Male) in 1990

87%

China (Male) in 200

95.1%

CHINA

China (Female) in 1990

68.1%

China (Female) in 200

86.5%

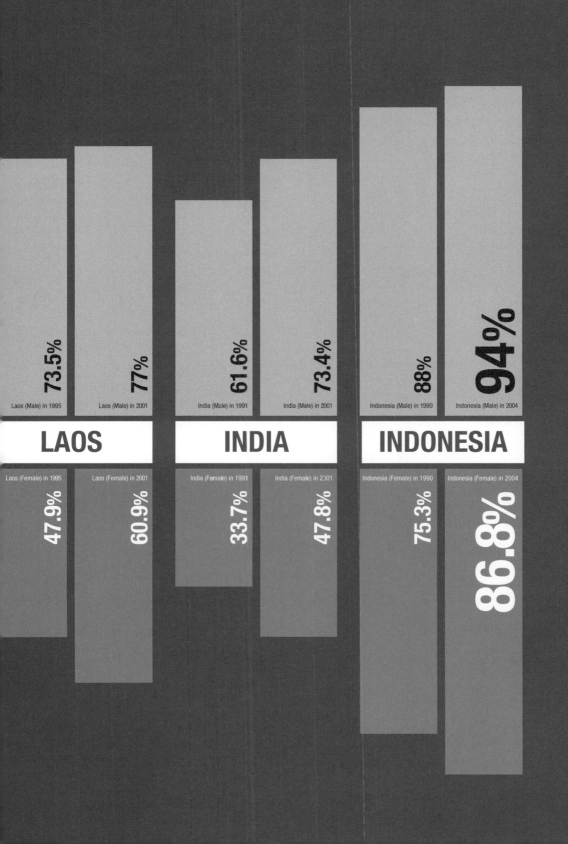

Laos (Male) in 1995 **73.5%**

Laos (Male) in 2001 **77%**

India (Male) in 1991 **61.6%**

India (Male) in 2001 **73.4%**

Indonesia (Male) in 1990 **88%**

Indonesia (Male) in 2004 **94%**

LAOS

INDIA

INDONESIA

Laos (Female) in 1995 **47.9%**

Laos (Female) in 2001 **60.9%**

India (Female) in 1991 **33.7%**

India (Female) in 2001 **47.8%**

Indonesia (Female) in 1990 **75.3%**

Indonesia (Female) in 2004 **86.8%**

Four of the world's fifteen best hotels are now in Asia; three in the top ten are in India, more than any other country except America.

MORE
5 STAR
HOTELS

HOTELS

8

14

1997

3

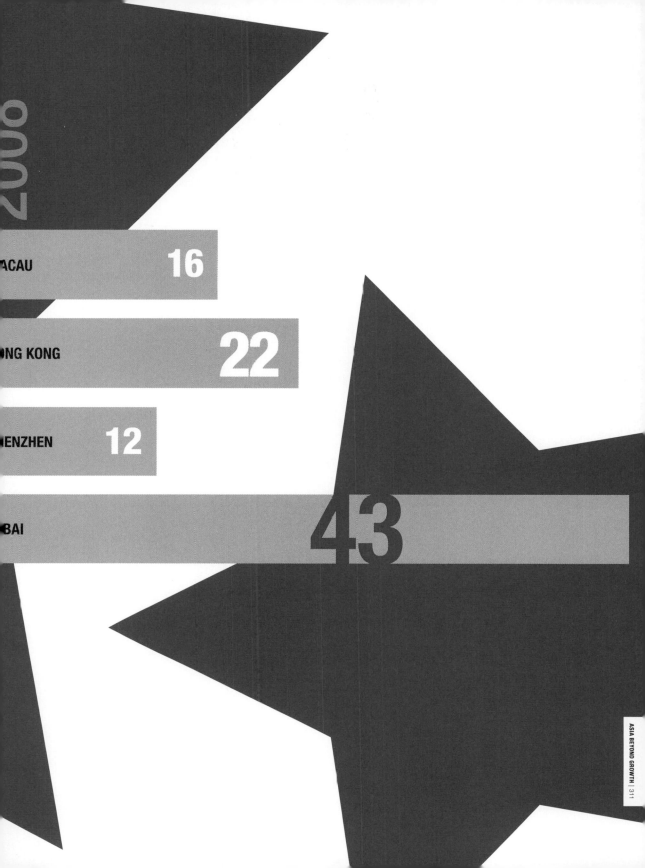

2006

ACAU 16

NG KONG 22

ENZHEN 12

BAI 43

Traditional food sources such as these ready-to-make stalls in Beijing are disappearing with an unprecedented infusion of foreign notions of food and beverage. As Asia's people become richer, their diets have changed more rapidly in a generation than throughout history.

MORE
BILLIONAIRES
In current USD.

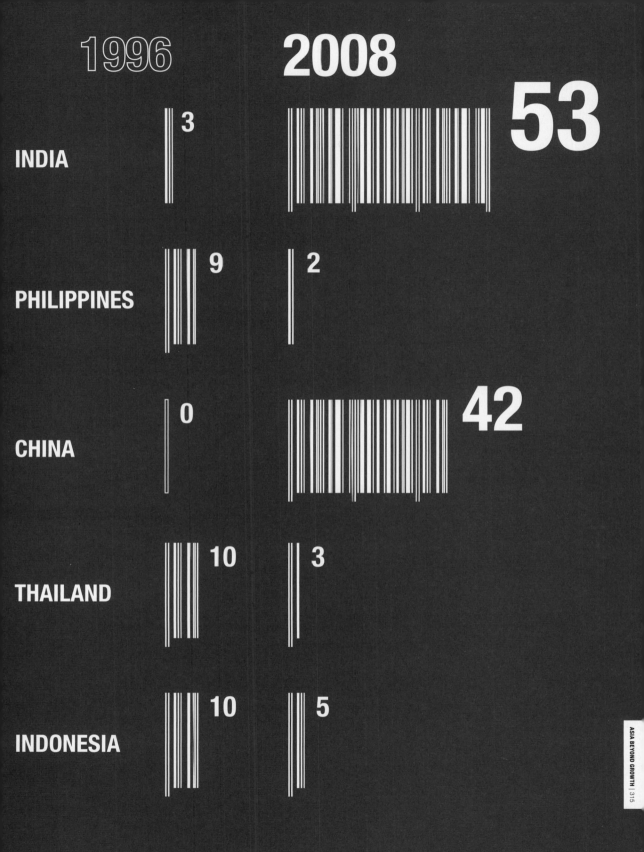

1996   2008

INDIA
3
53

PHILIPPINES
9
2

CHINA
0
42

THAILAND
10
3

INDONESIA
10
5

MORE
BILLIONAIRES

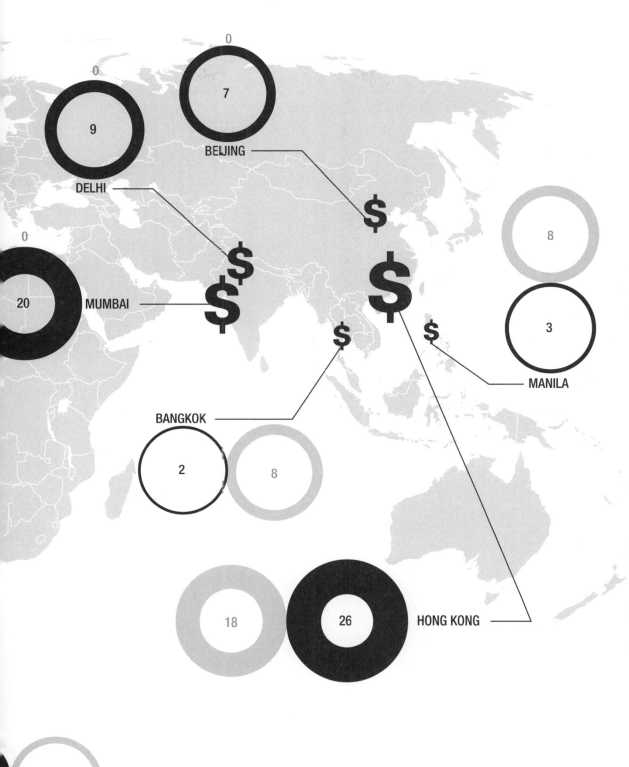

0

0

9

DELHI

0

20

MUMBAI

0

7

BEIJING

$

$

$

$

$

8

3

MANILA

$

BANGKOK

2

8

18

26

HONG KONG

1997

GROWING
FOREIGN DIRECT
INVESTMENT

Percentage growth in Foreign Direct Investment (FDI) the period from 1990-2006.

QATAR
11,952%

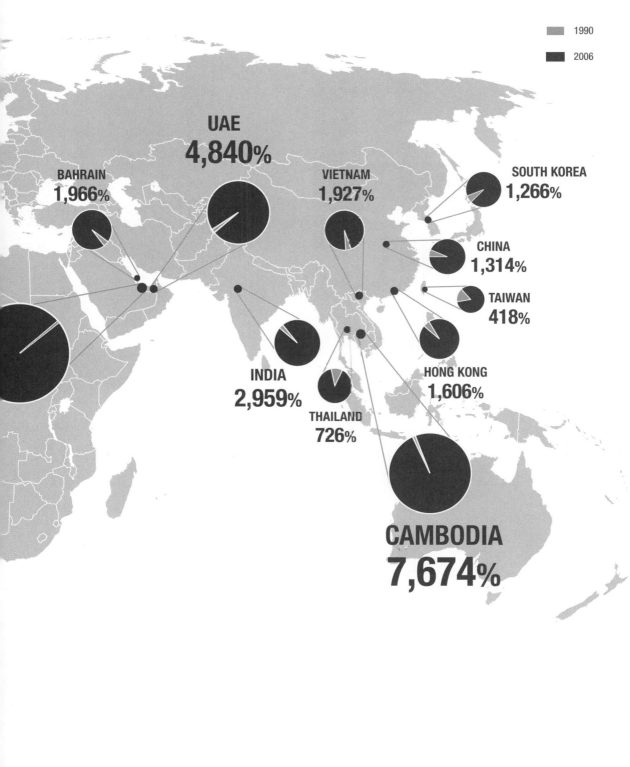

INDONESIA
5%

4.9%

GROWING
OBESITY

Percentage of total population that is obese.

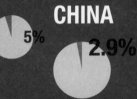

CHINA
2.9%

5%

SOUTH KOREA
13.2%

0.8%

180 200

220

WEIGHT 240

260

280

300

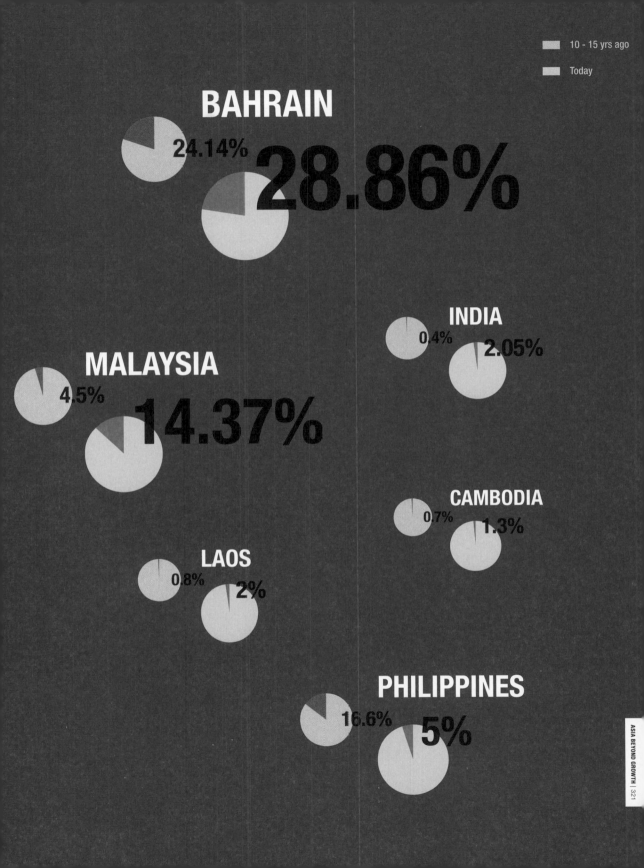

Of the world's ten largest shopping malls,
eight are in Asia.

欢迎

We

沃尔玛创始人——山姆·沃尔顿
Founder of Wal-Mart -- Sam Walton

中秋团圆　WAL★MART SUPERCENTER
沃尔玛购物广场　中秋团圆

天天平价

CHINA

HONG KONG

GROWING
FASHION

UAE   **INDIA**

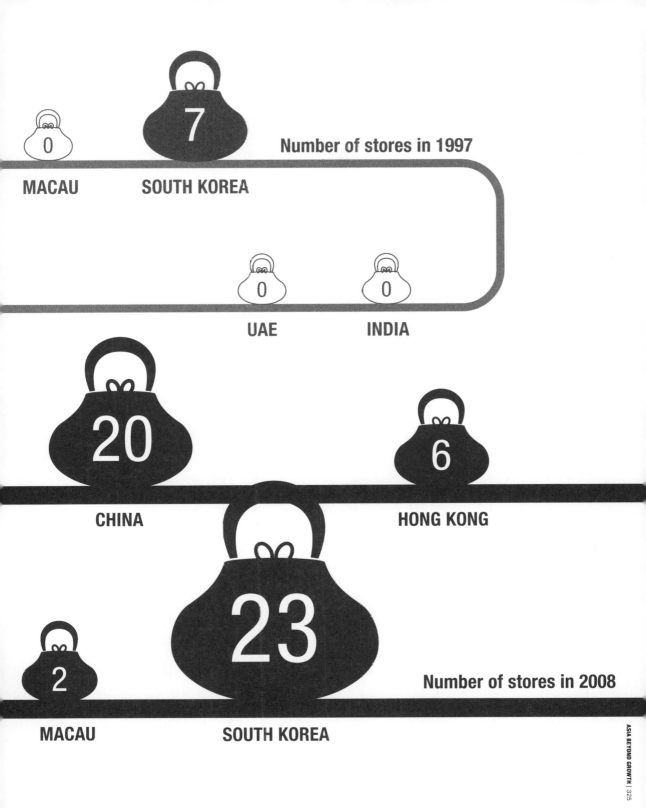

Number of stores in 1997

MACAU

SOUTH KOREA

UAE

INDIA

CHINA

HONG KONG

Number of stores in 2008

MACAU

SOUTH KOREA

Tesco 1997

🛒🛒🛒🛒🛒🛒🛒🛒🛒🛒🛒🛒🛒🛒🛒🛒🛒🛒🛒🛒 **0** CHINA
🛒🛒🛒🛒🛒🛒🛒🛒🛒🛒🛒🛒🛒🛒🛒🛒🛒🛒🛒🛒 **0** MALAYSIA
🛒🛒🛒🛒🛒🛒🛒🛒🛒🛒🛒🛒🛒🛒🛒🛒🛒🛒🛒🛒 **0** SOUTH KOREA
🛒🛒🛒🛒🛒🛒🛒🛒🛒🛒🛒🛒🛒🛒🛒🛒🛒🛒🛒🛒 **0** THAILAND

Tesco 2008

🛒🛒🛒🛒🛒🛒🛒🛒🛒🛒🛒🛒🛒🛒🛒🛒🛒🛒🛒🛒 **47** CHINA
🛒🛒🛒🛒🛒🛒🛒🛒🛒🛒🛒🛒🛒🛒🛒🛒🛒🛒🛒🛒 **19** MALAYSIA
🛒🛒🛒🛒🛒🛒🛒🛒🛒🛒🛒🛒🛒🛒🛒🛒🛒🛒🛒🛒 **81** SOUTH KOREA
🛒🛒🛒🛒🛒🛒🛒🛒🛒🛒🛒🛒🛒🛒🛒🛒🛒🛒🛒🛒 **370** THAILAND

Walmart 1997

🛒🛒🛒🛒🛒🛒🛒🛒🛒🛒🛒🛒🛒🛒🛒🛒🛒🛒🛒🛒 **2** CHINA

Walmart 2008

🛒🛒🛒🛒🛒🛒🛒🛒🛒🛒🛒🛒🛒🛒🛒🛒🛒🛒🛒🛒 **203** CHINA

Tesco   Walmart

SUPERSTORES

= 20

Carrefour 1997

	Count	Country
	15	CHINA
	3	INDONESIA
	5	MALAYSIA
	0	OMAN
	0	QATAR
	21	TAIWAN
	7	THAILAND
	1	UAE

Carrefour 2008

	Count	Country
	122	CHINA
	37	INDONESIA
	12	MALAYSIA
	2	OMAN
	3	QATAR
	48	TAIWAN
	25	THAILAND
	11	UAE

Carrefours SUPERSTORES

BEYOND RETAIL: TRANSFORMING HEARTS, MINDS, AND PLACE

The picture of the underbelly of China's feverish development is a consistently grim one: anonymous crowded public space divorced from its heritage, yellow, hazy skies, toxic water.

Our masterplan for Shuibei offers a new way forward for emerging Chinese cities. Synthesizing local materials, hard-scapes, planting, colors, and cultural references, our design solutions demonstrate how we can re-invigorate the identities of ancient cities in a contemporary context.

By invoking colloquial vernacular symbols we created a new paradigm in cultural and urban renewal in China and beyond; in the end the project demonstrates how the cultural resources of cities can pay dividends in re-vitalization and help preserve the historical dignity of place for future generations.

SHINING UP THE JEWELS

Located in the heart of the booming border city of Shenzhen, Shuibei is a 68 hectare parcel of land in the city's central Louhu District, several kilometers from the Lowu border checkpoint between Mainland China and Hong Kong. The area plays a prominent role in the regional jewelry industry and houses a high concentration of jewelers and jewelry manufacturers, numbering some 300 different

SHUIBEI ILLUSTRATES HOW WE CAN TRANSFORM BOTH THE HEARTS AND MINDS OF PEOPLE AND, MORE SIGNIFICANTLY, THE URBAN PUBLIC REALM ITSELF. BY INVOKING THE LOCAL HERITAGE, WE QUIETLY HELPED SHUIBEI BECOME SHUIBEI AGAIN.

jewelry-related businesses. While Shuibei is responsible for a quarter of China's jewelry output, the area lacks luster with a disorderly appearance, the heavy impact of manufacturing on the surrounding atmosphere, and a number of dilapidated structures, a low quality residential offer and an overall deficit in character.

We were brought in by Shenzhen's planning authorities to devise a new strategy for the neighborhood's future direction while cementing its identity as a regional center for creativity in and production of jewelry. Shui Bei District urban revitalization will enable Shenzhen's

TWO NEW PUBLIC SQUARES ARE INSERTED INTO THE EXISTING MILIEU, INJECTING DIVERSITY INTO THE EXISTING STREET GRID, WHICH IS ALSO INTEGRATED WITH THE REMAINDER OF THE CITY WHERE BARRIERS CURRENTLY EXIST.

Jewelry industry to mature into its next phase of development by becoming a destination offering high quality manufacturing, exhibition, and hotel facilities for the trade, educational facilities for Design schools, while adding new retail and entertainment environments to the public. Our urban revitalization provided historical and cultural framework, economic business development, and humanized a vibrant public realm.

HISTORIC & CULTURAL PRESERVATION

The master plan begins with Shuibei Number One Road, converting this underutilized artery for the district into a vibrant commercial street with provision for more commercial and mixed-use development along the street. Factory zones are cleaned up and integrated with exhibition and retail spaces, enhancing their appeal for visitors. At the key intersection of Cuizhu Road and Shuibei Number One Road, which acts as a gateway for the quarter, commerce and culture come together with a new retail center and a museum/convention facility.

The plan also addresses Shuibei's architectural character with an integrated approach that balances preservation of existing structures and character with the need for new expression and spaces. The needs of all stakeholders are addressed in a careful and holistic way – local authorities will be able to market the area's specific appeal for tourism, residents will have a fresher and cleaner environment and Shuibei's jewelry industry will be enhanced. Our regenerative plan is one that will preserve the grain and scale of Shuibei, will improve the quality of its built environment and will raise the tenor of community by building upon its existing identity and cultural resources, as well as existing damage to the natural environment.

JEWELRY INDUSTRY AND TOURISM DEVELOPMENT

The main feature of the plan is the "Shuibei Necklace", a system of pedestrian walkways and courtyards that string together the redevelopment opportunities in the area, creating a commercial and retail environment unique to the industry and a special new destination for the city.

JEWELRY SHOPS, SHOWROOMS AND TOURISM PROGRAMS ARE STRUNG ALONG THIS NECKLACE LIKE GEMS – CREATING A DYNAMIC SYNERGY.

Anchor programs include a 5-star hotel, a conference center, a retail mall, and a design institute. This plan calls for the improvement of 370,000 square meters of space and construction of 176,000 square meters of new production, office and tourism facilities.

IT IS A DEMONSTRATIVE EXERCISE IN URBAN RENEWAL THAT HAS MINIMAL DESTRUCTION AND PRESERVES THE EXISTING GRAIN AND SCALE OF A CITY – BOTH A RARITY IN THE BURGEONING CONTEXT OF THE CONTEMPORARY CHINESE CITY.

RENOVATION NOT DEMOLITION

The first phase of the master plan's implementation, which is complete, offers a model for improving Shenzhen's overall built environment in a way that is affordable and unobtrusive. An award such as this one and at this juncture would do much to encourage a rapidly growing city to continue its efforts to better a predominately unattractive public realm, which is at its very core, home to millions of people. This first realization shows the power of urban clean-up, and is helping to not just regenerate a neighborhood but also provides a more lustrous home for a local creative industry. In the time since this phase has opened, property values have increased significantly. To make this all happen, government teamed with local industry, and has had a generous return on its investment.

For these reasons, it should be commended. The needs of all stakeholders are addressed in a careful and holistic way – local authorities have been able to market the area's specific appeal for a creative industry while generating revenue at relatively low cost, residents have a fresher and cleaner environment and the local jewelry industry has an enhanced public sphere. This regenerative plan is a sensible one that raises the tenor of a community without altering its existing identity.

NEW MODEL FOR NEIGHBORHOOD REGENERATIVE AND AN EMERGING CREATIVE INDUSTRY

Within the completed area, there are six main structures, three of which frame a dramatic new public square. These buildings are a combination of cleaned-up and enhanced industrial buildings and new architecture that carefully blends with the older structures. The new square is a focus point for public

WITHIN THE GRIT OF SHUIBEI NOW, THERE IS A PLACE THAT CELEBRATES AN EMERGING CREATIVE CULTURE, HAS PRODUCED SUCCESSFUL FINANCIAL RESULTS FOR BOTH THE PUBLIC PRIVATE SECTORS, AND HAS DONE SO WITH COMPARATIVELY LITTLE INTERFERENCE IN THE NEIGHBORHOODS EXISTING BUILT ENVIRONMENT.

events and has an al fresco atmosphere set in contemporary, artistically-interesting landscaping that is a rare site in the general vicinity. This public square is perpendicular to a large open pedestrianized promenade that links the buildings around ample open spaces, which act as courtyards. Financially this project has been a win-win for the local government, which took on an investment role in the scheme.

The result is a new model for grounded, site-sensitive, economically viable conversions of manufacturing-based neighborhoods. It is a model that should inspire the future direction of many other similar industrial urban contexts in China, Asia and beyond.

MO

CONNECTIONS

As more and more people fly to and within the Emerging World, its airports are getting bigger, and its airlines are getting better. The world's best 5 airports and 8 of the 10 best airlines are all on the continent of Asia.

CA Air China

Main Hub: BEIJING

6.2

Average new destinations
pr year since founded
in 1988

EK Emirates

Main Hub: DUBAI

4.22 Average new destinations pr year since founded in 1985

CX Cathay Pacific

Main Hub: HONG KONG

1.69 Average new destinations pr year since founded in 1946

— Air China destinations in 2008

— Cathay Pacific Airways destinations when founded in 1946
— Cathay Pacific Airways destinations in 2008
— Dragon Airline destinations in 2008

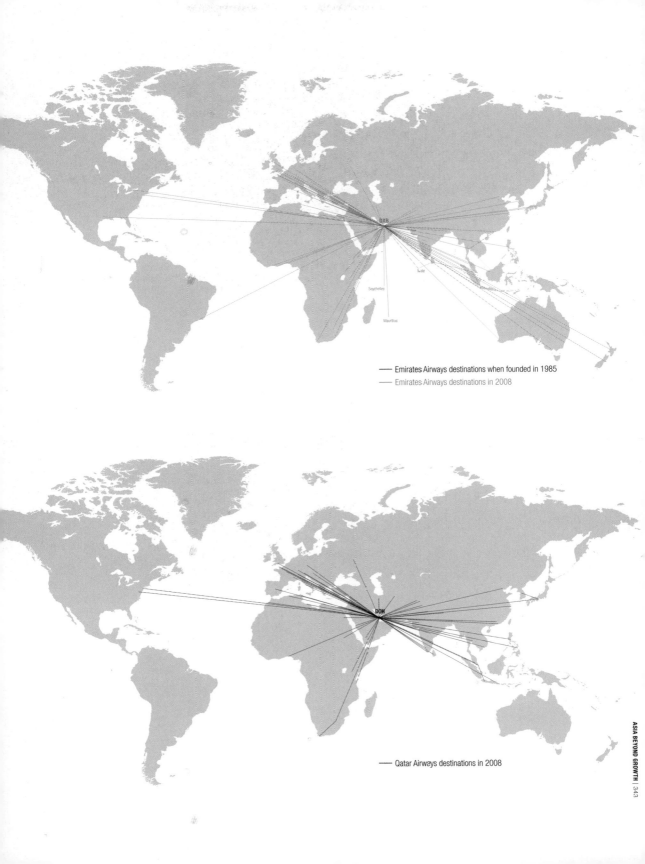

Emirates Airways destinations when founded in 1985

Emirates Airways destinations in 2008

Qatar Airways destinations in 2008

HORIZONTAL, DIAGONAL, VERTICAL: LAYERING THE LANDSCAPE OF AN ISLAND METROPOLIS

Hong Kong. Asia's Manhattan, a city of seven million, it has one of the highest urban densities in the world. Born of a perfect harbor, like New York, it evolved from a colonial trading port into the dominant center of international finance and commerce in the Eastern Hemisphere. In both cities, skyscrapers became a principal instrument of economic growth and have multiplied into incomparable, iconic skylines. The urban dynamic of vertical density is a model that was established in Manhattan in the early twentieth century and has been reproduced in Hong Kong since the 1970s with sometimes dizzyingly surreal results. A forest of towers standing against the mountain is the image that comes to mind when we describe the multi-layered urban landscape that evolved in Hong Kong during the post-war period, and continued its miraculous mutation into what we see today.

Today, Hong Kong surpasses New York in the number of high-rises, hyper-dense habitation, and efficient mass transit. Apartment towers commonly rise fifty to sixty stories or taller, even in surrounding new towns. Densities of 90,000 or more people per square mile – well above Manhattan's average of 70,000 – are typical.

In its newest high-rise hubs, Hong Kong realizes aspects of the dreams of a rationalized city of towers that New York architects envisioned in the 1920s.

Paradoxically, for a city as large, densely populated and urbanized as Hong Kong, the rapid public transport system was developed late in comparison with other modern metropolises such as Tokyo, Paris or New York.

MTR, THE MOST RECOGNIZED BRAND IN HONG KONG

After commissioning a study in the 1960s to find solutions to the growing traffic problem caused by the expansion of the city's economy, construction started on the MTR, a local mass transit rail system, with the first line opening in 1979.

Due to its efficiency and affordability, the MTR system is a common mode of public transport in Hong Kong, with over 4 million trips made in an average weekday. The integration of smart card fare-payment technology – the Octopus Card – into the MTR system in September 1997 has further enhanced the ease of commuting on through the layers of the island metropolis.

The MTR was immediately popular with residents of Hong Kong; as a result, subsequent lines have been built to cover more territory. The MTR first began service officially merged with the Kowloon Canton Railway (KCR) on 2 December 2007, still bearing the same name in English. The network

HONG KONG'S EXTREME URBANISM IS DISTINGUISHED BY ITS CROWDED COMMERCIAL CORE, ITS MULTI-LEVEL TRAFFIC AND SYSTEM OF PEDESTRIAN BRIDGES, ITS UNIQUELY SLENDER BUILDINGS, VERTICAL SHOPPING MALLS, MASSIVE HOUSING ESTATES, LUXURY APARTMENTS, AND SIGNATURE SKYSCRAPERS.

includes 211.6 kilometers of rail with 150 stations, including 82 railway stations and 68 light rail stops.

The MTR also connects with the Airport Express, a quick and comfortable train that departs at 12-minute intervals to and from the Hong Kong Airport from several points within the city. The Hong Kong Airport is probably the best connected and most efficient airport in the world. Even the airport has layers – people arriving on one level – people departing on another level.

ARCHITECTURE MERGING WITH PUBLIC REALM

The best example of how the city's infrastructure merges with buildings is in the Mass-transit stations and they are integrated within shopping centers (the reason for this is the collaboration between the MTR and property developers). Pedestrian movement systems merge with architecture; Hong Kong's footbridge system is a hybrid between a walkway and a public space. On Sundays domestic maids use the footbridges as a public space but on weekdays they're used for pedestrian circulation.

A NEW KIND OF TRANSIT: THE MID-LEVELS ESCALATOR

Since its completion in 1994, the Mid-Level escalators have transformed the Central/Soho neighborhoods they transverse into a popular arts and restaurant district. Despite their functional aesthetic the escalators create a unique cross sectional view of the city and have become a place of sight seeing and people watching. With the escalators recent expansion to connect to a series of shopping malls, the ferry terminal and new office buildings it is possible to commute to work, go shopping, visit restaurants and travel back home without ever leaving a covered enclosure.

PUBLIC FOOTBRIDGES, CENTRAL, HONG KONG

SOMEHOW WE'VE COME TO EQUATE PEDESTRIAN ESCALATORS WITH AIRLESS UTOPIAN MODERNIST CITIES WHERE CONVEYOR BELTS FERRET LONE FIGURES THROUGH AN EVENTLESS URBAN LANDSCAPE. BUT IN HONG KONG, THESE ESCALATORS SEEM TO HAVE FOSTERED QUITE A ROBUST PUBLIC SPACE.

The world's longest outdoor escalator that snakes up above the steep, narrow streets of Hong Kong Island connects the urban grid to slender towers that soar high above. Together with the elevated pedestrian bridges that link the lower-level floors of a series of towers in the financial district, the escalator portrays an exciting horizontal, and even diagonal, connectivity.

The escalator system was conceived to alleviate car traffic by helping commuters travel efficiently to work while providing protection from rain. They have proven to be very popular, carrying over 45,000 people a day.

Somehow we've come to equate pedestrian escalators with airless utopian modernist city where conveyor belts ferret lone figures through an eventless urban landscape. But in Hong Kong, these escalators seem to have fostered quite a robust public space.

Adding a layer to the busy street level and underground transit systems, it activates the otherwise cut-off verticality: a successful prototype in practice that cries for further investigation in the designs for future cities all around the world. Hong Kong thus becomes a complex system in continual transformation: the intersection of people, transport,

MID-LEVELS ESCALATOR, SOHO, HONG KONG

HONG KONG THUS BECOMES A COMPLEX SYSTEM IN CONTINUAL TRANSFORMATION: THE INTERSECTION OF PEOPLE, TRANSPORT, FLOWS, MUTATIONS, MOVEMENT, ENERGIES, AND CROSSROADS. INDEED, THERE IS NO RIGID DEMARCATION BETWEEN WHAT IS PRIVATE AND PUBLIC AND NO STRONG PSYCHOLOGICAL DEMARCATION BETWEEN ONE PIECE OF ARCHITECTURE AND THE NEXT. AS A RESULT, HONG KONG HAS SOME THE MOST DYNAMIC PUBLIC SPACES IN THE WORLD.

flows, mutations, movement, energies, and crossroads. Indeed, there is no rigid demarcation between what is private and public and no strong psychological demarcation between one piece of architecture and the next. As a result, Hong Kong has some the most dynamic public spaces in the world.

POSITIVES AND NEGATIVES OF HONG KONG'S DENSITY

Hong Kong is a user-friendly, pedestrian-friendly city, something that cities like Beijing or Los Angeles could learn from. This compactness produces a vibrant diverse mix. You have living zones very close to commercial zones. You have markets, sometimes literally, downstairs. You are within walking distance of shops, bars, and restaurants.

On the other hand, in order to achieve this density, some very basic humans concerns are neglected. You have to be able to stand the noise. Privacy can be a problem. And sometimes this density creates a "wall" effect, blocking the winds from the sea and worsening pollution.

CHALLENGES FOR THE FUTURE

The main challenge is to find an intelligent balance between sustainability concerns and issues of density and compactness. The Government is responding to environmental groups and downscaling development sites. But there is a danger that the pendulum is swinging too much the other way too fast. There is also the danger that by drastically reducing the density of our city, we might lose our original strength, that we are walkable and connectable.

WITH ITS CREATIVE DYNAMIC USE OF THE MULTI-TEXTURED PUBLIC REALM, PERHAPS HONG KONG CAN ACT AS A BLUEPRINT IN HOW OTHER CITIES REDUCE HORIZONTAL SPRAWL AND PURSUE EFFICIENT, INTELLIGENT LAND USE AS A CRITICAL STRATEGY FOR SUSTAINABLE DEVELOPMENT.

MODEL FOR REDUCING HORIZONTAL SPRAWL

2008 is the first year in history in which the majority of the world population lives in cities. Lightning urbanization (by 2050 the world population will grow by three billion, with two billion living in urbanized areas) calls for new thinking about better ways to design infrastructure and fabric of cities. With its creative dynamic use of the multi-textured public realm, perhaps Hong Kong can act as a blueprint in how other cities reduce horizontal sprawl and pursue efficient, intelligent land use as a critical strategy for sustainable development.

MIRACULOUS MUTATION

Hong Kong is still in the midst of a miraculous mutation. It can have a fundamental and lasting influence on how we can reduce horizontal sprawl and further integrate cities in the coming decades. The successfully integrated city thrives by celebrating what makes a place unique and builds upon it's organic strengths: diversity, dynamism, creativity, cultural exchange and human interconnectivity between people and places and transportation.

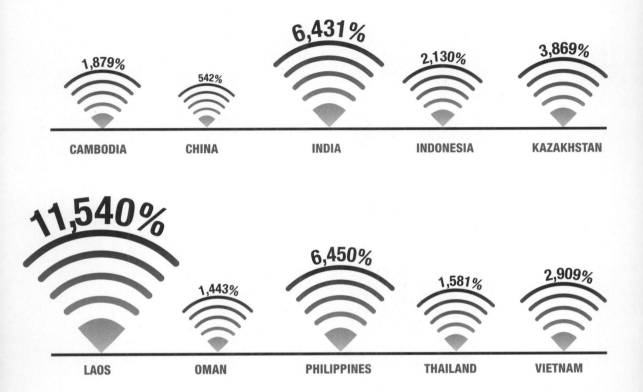

1,879%
CAMBODIA

542%
CHINA

6,431%
INDIA

2,130%
INDONESIA

3,869%
KAZAKHSTAN

11,540%
LAOS

1,443%
OMAN

6,450%
PHILIPPINES

1,581%
THAILAND

2,909%
VIETNAM

GROWING
MOBILE PHONE USE

Percentage increase since 2000.

Mobile phones per capita - top 4 countries/territories worldwide in 2007.

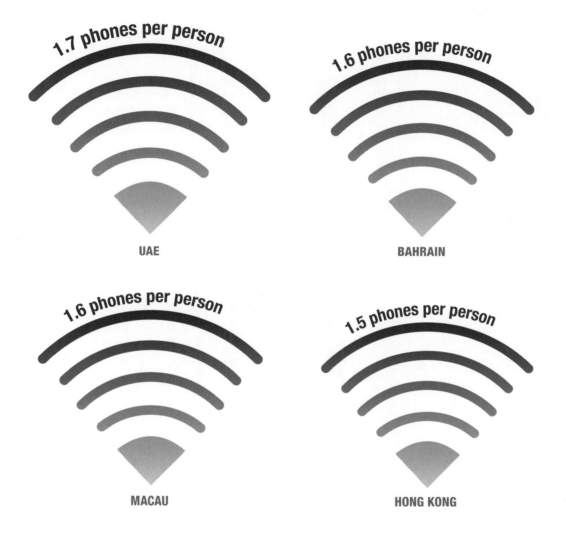

1.7 phones per person
UAE

1.6 phones per person
BAHRAIN

1.6 phones per person
MACAU

1.5 phones per person
HONG KONG

CO

MOPOLITANISM

DRAGON LAKE BRIDGE PARK: A SHORT STORY OF EMPERORS, WATER AND THE SPIRIT OF TRANSFORMATION

As legend has it, a young boy set out to pole his boat on the shallow waters of China's Anhui province. When the small vessel capsized and immersed the child into the waters, he arose as a splendid dragon. This peasant boy, named Zhu Yuanzhang, later became the founder and first emperor of the Ming Dynasty, reigning from 1368 to 1398. The lake where this mystical transformation took place has since been named Longzi, or Dragon Lake, which lies adjacent to the burgeoning city of Bengbu.

By 2008, Bengbu's residents awoke to a beautiful lakeside surprise: after two years of construction, the south part of Dragon Lake Bridge Park opened, ushering yet another transformation – albeit a slightly less magical one – into the local lore. For the first time in memory, Bengbu's lakefront became accessible and the city's first contemporary park was opened; a public domain that reflects as much on tradition and the local color of Bengbu as it embraces the city's recent development by creating a new, modern face of the city towards the lake. In this respect, the new park reintegrates the lakefront into the life of the city, and instills a great sense of civic pride among the citizens of Bengbu.

The new lakeside park is the first achievement of a mutual effort of the State Land Planning Bureau of Bengbu's New City Comprehensive Development Zone, the Shanghai Xiandai Architectural Design Group and AECOM's Design + Planning practice, which initiated the project in 2005 with the strategic master plan that is guiding the long-term evolution of the entire 39.8-square kilometer lakeside from a neglected asset at the city fringe into a central scenic spot and community focus for the expanding city.

In Chinese, Bengbu translates into Clam Wharf, echoing the city's heritage as a freshwater pearl fishery. As the name suggests, the city's relationship with the adjacent body of water is the key component of both Bengbu's origins and character. In recent years, however, Bengbu's connection to its waterside has waned significantly as it has faced tremendous changes due to China's hyper-development. Rapid industrial development and urbanization have taken a stark toll on both Bengbu's urban environment and the water supply for the entire county (population: 3.49 million), which has been further endangered by the delayed completion of an urban sewage network and wastewater treatment facilities. Over time, Dragon Lake became eutrophic, and its water quality has deteriorated to a point to which human contact with the water is no longer recommended.

Meanwhile, the City of Bengbu itself – with a population of roughly 600,000 – has undergone tremendous evolution. Bengbu's economy, which has historically been driven by agriculture, aquaculture, food processing and low-skill manufacturing, has matured dramatically in recent years as China's coastal economic growth spread inwards. The economy in present day Bengbu is shifting away from agriculture towards light manufacturing and secondary and tertiary industries. Economic growth has led to urbanization and a growing number of people with relatively higher incomes. The city is growing up. This has caused the city to expand towards the east, a move which has brought it closer to the lake and will – according to proposed city extensions – begin to encircle the lake in phases, changing Dragon Lake from a natural area at the city's edge into a central feature of the urban landscape.

The recent changes in Bengbu are reflective of the broad pattern of socio-economic upheaval that has been occurring in many small and medium- sized regional cities in China. The country's rapid urbanization has unleashed the largest internal migration in the history of mankind, with an estimated 100 to 150 million people moving from the countryside to the city in the last 15 years. This process is still ongoing and is now focused towards second and third tier regional cities, where housing and cost-of-living are still affordable for lower income groups. The rising economy has also led to a growing middle class, which has a newfound appreciation for a green, sustainable living environment, as well as the need for recreational spaces. This is why many regional cities in China have reached a critical stage in their development, in which they find themselves having to invest in the quality of the overall urban environment, in order to stay competitive in attracting business

BENGBU'S ECONOMY, WHICH HAS HISTORICALLY BEEN DRIVEN BY AGRICULTURE, AQUACULTURE, FOOD PROCESSING AND LOW-SKILL MANUFACTURING, HAS MATURED DRAMATICALLY IN RECENT YEARS AS CHINA'S COASTAL ECONOMIC GROWTH SPREAD INWARDS.

and talent, and in enhancing property values. This requires a strong, clear and recognizable identity compared with other cities that can only be achieved through investment in improving the city's physical and natural environments in a way that speaks to the aspirations of new middle classes and the interest in green living. For China, this is a new phenomenon which is showing some promising results, nowhere more than in the relatively unknown city of Bengbu.

What Bengbu needed was a facelift. The master plan identifies three major objectives in order to achieve this: first, the improvement of water quality as a key landscape design aim; secondly, the enrichment of cultural and recreational offerings available to the larger community; and lastly, the establishment of a new lake district and a signature lakeside park at its western shore that provides a meaningful interface between the city and lake; the core upon which to develop a progressive lakeside city.

The role of water quality thus became paramount in the considerations of the landscape architects. A thorough, long-term improvement in the water quality to a level that allows for human contact was thought to tremendously enhance the attractiveness and recreational potential of the lake. However, the issues of poor water quality and ecosystem stability had to be addressed

on a watershed-wide basis in order to realize the goal of a clean lake and an attractive natural environment. Within the perimeter of the site, a variety of closely interrelated hydrological and ecological measures was suggested, including artificial circulation and aeration of the lake by regular submerged injections of compressed air during the dry and warm months; the reduction of hydraulic retention time through the implementation of a new hydrologic scheme involving supplemental water from the nearby Tian Lake and treated wastewater; construction of wetlands for treatment of tertiary wastewater; restoration of stream channels and vegetated riparian buffers; habitat improvements to establish a balance between the aquatic, riparian and upland ecosystems, ranging from cold water refugia to isolated islands within the lake; floodplain restoration reaching wildlife corridors; and the reforestation of upper preserves.

These measures not only enhance the natural environment but also reintroduce the character of the vernacular landscape, providing Dragon Lake with a distinct and genuine landscape that can accommodate a variety of recreational and cultural facilities. By extension, a connection to historical antecedents is restored to the city itself. A string of attractions encircles the lake to create a diverse series of sites reflecting and celebrating cultural heritage as well as

introducing educational facilities such as wildlife centers, areas for green farming, local and regional sport amenities.

Developments in China happen quickly. After completing the master plan, the city commissioned the design of the first stage of the central lakeside park, the Lake Bridge Park, which comprises a total of 25 hectares of new public open space. The new park is located around an important transit corridor, the newly built Dragon Lake Bridge, the main east-west artery of Bengbu and the western gateway to the city center. In acknowledgement of this built incision into the lake, the design of Lake Bridge Park reflects on the nature of the lake in an urban way. The original topography has been translated into a terraced landscape, allowing for a continuous flow of visitors alongside the lake, while a succession of urban nodes links the waterside promenade with the city and thereby activates and orchestrates the lakeside.

Each stage of the project posed its very own design challenges. At the level of the concrete design, it was necessary to convince the client to apply the basic design principles stated in the landscape framework. Alongside the urban edge of the lake, local plant species were selected rather than exotic plantings in order to anchor

THESE MEASURES NOT ONLY ENHANCE THE NATURAL ENVIRONMENT BUT ALSO REINTRODUCE THE CHARACTER OF THE VERNACULAR LANDSCAPE, PROVIDING DRAGON LAKE WITH A DISTINCT AND GENUINE LANDSCAPE THAT CAN ACCOMMODATE A VARIETY OF RECREATIONAL AND CULTURAL FACILITIES.

the site in its natural context and provide a continuous habitat network. This localism and ecological sensibility were further achieved by deploying low-impact design principles, like the use of multi-modes of energy-saving lighting for example, and by drawing on traditional methods for the structural design of architectural components, such as the use of traditional retaining walls found in terraces and pavilions.

Another challenge was embedded in the chosen design language itself. The defining question for the designers became how to create a unique and genuine waterfront, which clearly reflects the spirit and character of Bengbu, while honoring both its tradition as much as its future potential. What is an adequate expression of landscape architecture that is both contemporary yet distinctly Chinese? The designers addressed these questions by trying to convey the spirit of the Chinese landscape and by searching for a contemporary equivalent rather than interpreting and transforming traditional shapes and configurations which has been much iterated in other cities. The Bamboo Garden and the Celebration Plaza, which form the core of the Lake Bridge Park, are fine examples of this approach. The Bamboo Garden takes a local feature, the dense bamboo forest, and transforms it in the simple move of expanding the spacing

between the stalks into an imaginative grove, playing on the fascination of ever broken visual lines. Chinese gardens are about landscape and the imagination of landscape, full of symbols and allegories, and this practice is extended into the Celebration Plaza, which exploits this capacity of decomposition and imagination by using magnified sun shelters as landmarks and a metaphor inscribing the shapes of openings into the sky.

This first, southern part of the park opened in December 2007 and has proved a success best evidenced by the enthusiasm and civic pride of its visitors. As the northern part nears completion, and while work is being carried out on the detailed design of the next phase of this lakeside domain a gem-like landscape is gently taking form in Bengbu, allowing this emerging city to re-imagine its vernacular qualities.

This essay originally appeared in *Topos, Number 65.*

Dubai residents who are foreign-born

85%

Largest nationality in Dubai

INDIAN

Foreign tourist arrivals in INDIA in 2007

4,000,000

Foreign tourist arrivals in INDIA in 2000

2,640,000

60,000

Expatriates on full working
permits in SHANGHAI in 2007

4,000

Expatriates on full working
permits in SHANGHAI in 2000

40,000

Expatriate workers in INDIA in 2007

Households that receive Chinese state television outside China

45,000,000

Households in Asia that receive British state television

35,000,000

Households in Asia that receive French state television

17,000,000

= 2

= 2

Starbucks outlets in Shanghai

39

Costa Coffee outlets in Dubai

53

The Emerging World is young. In China, 560 million people are under the age of 20; in India, more than 41% of the population is under the age of 34.

MORE
EDUCATION

Students enrolled in domestic universities.

9%
PHILIPPINES
2,208,635 in 1999
2,402,649 in 2006

267%
CHINA
6,365,625 in 1999
23,360,535 in 2006

29%
THAILAND
1,814,096 in 1999
2,338,572 in 2006

67%
VIETNAM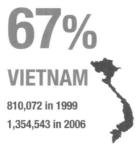
810,072 in 1999
1,354,543 in 2006

25%
INDIA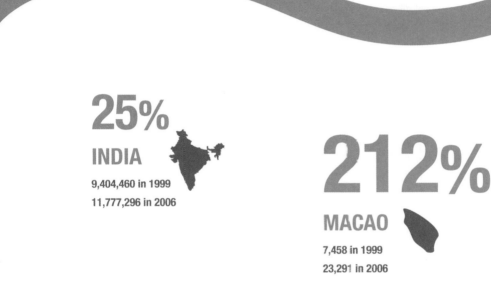
9,404,460 in 1999
11,777,296 in 2006

212%
MACAO
7,458 in 1999
23,291 in 2006

293%
LAOS
12,076 in 1999
47,424 in 2006

MORE
EDUCATION

Enrollment overseas by country/territory.

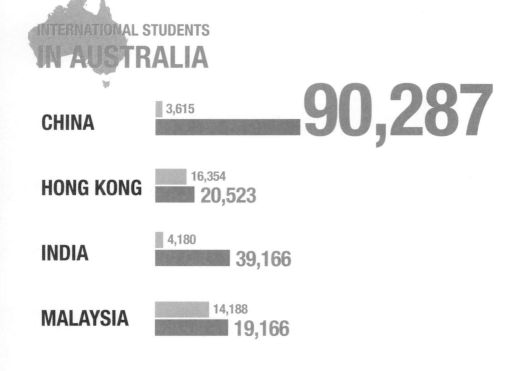

INTERNATIONAL STUDENTS
IN AUSTRALIA

CHINA
3,615
90,287

HONG KONG
16,354
20,523

INDIA
4,180
39,166

MALAYSIA
14,188
19,166

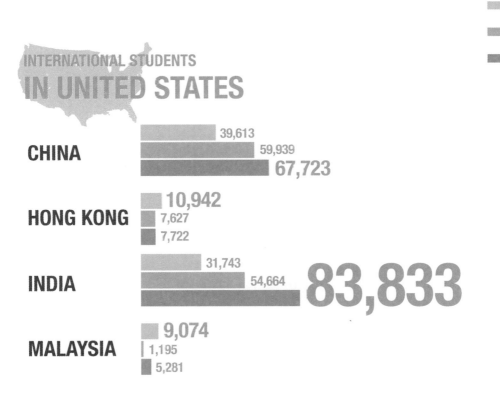

INTERNATIONAL STUDENTS

IN UNITED STATES

CHINA
39,613
59,939
67,723

HONG KONG
10,942
7,627
7,722

INDIA
31,743
54,664
83,833

MALAYSIA
9,074
1,195
5,281

INTERNATIONAL STUDENTS

IN UNITED KINGDOM

CHINA
N/A
12,095
50,755

HONG KONG
7,767
8,335
9,445

INDIA
2,302
4,875
19,205

MALAYSIA
18,015
10,005
11,450

GROWING
TOURIST ARRIVALS

Growth in foreign tourist arrivals in the period 1990-2005.

346%
CHINA

1,287%
VIETNAM

4,700%
LAOS

8,265%
CAMBODIA

259%
MACAU

118%
THAILAND

156%
PHILIPPINES

SOC

L INTEGRATION

IT'S ALL
ABOUT PEOPLE

In Asian cities, it is common for people to use the spaces between buildings as outdoor living rooms.
The public realm is commonly the venue for conversation, for meals, for a nap and for commerce.
In many places, it seems, all pieces of the city are used for and by people.

IN BEIJING

IN BANGKOK

IN HANGZHOU

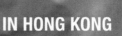

IN HONG KONG

IN BEIJING

IN DUBAI

IN MUMBAI

IN DUBAI AND HONG KONG

IN BANGKOK

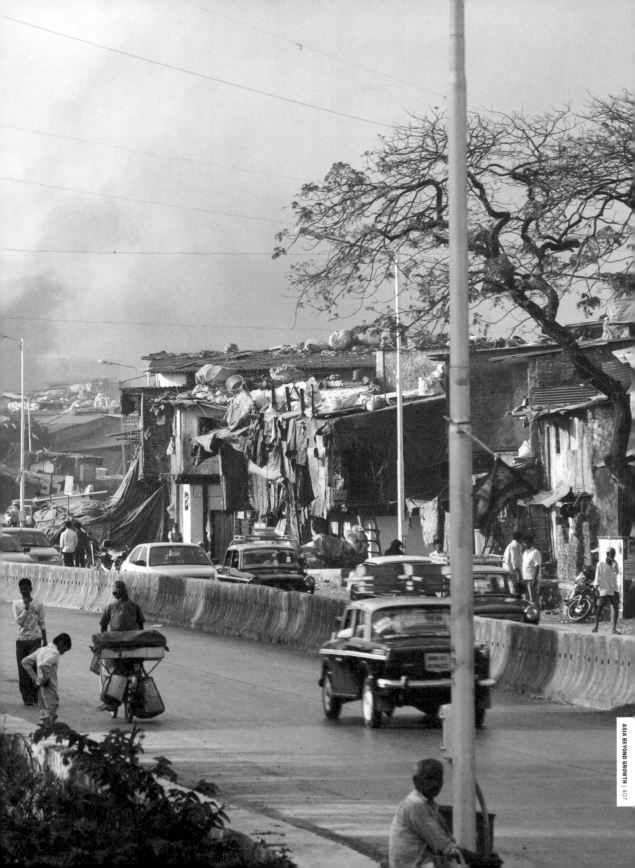

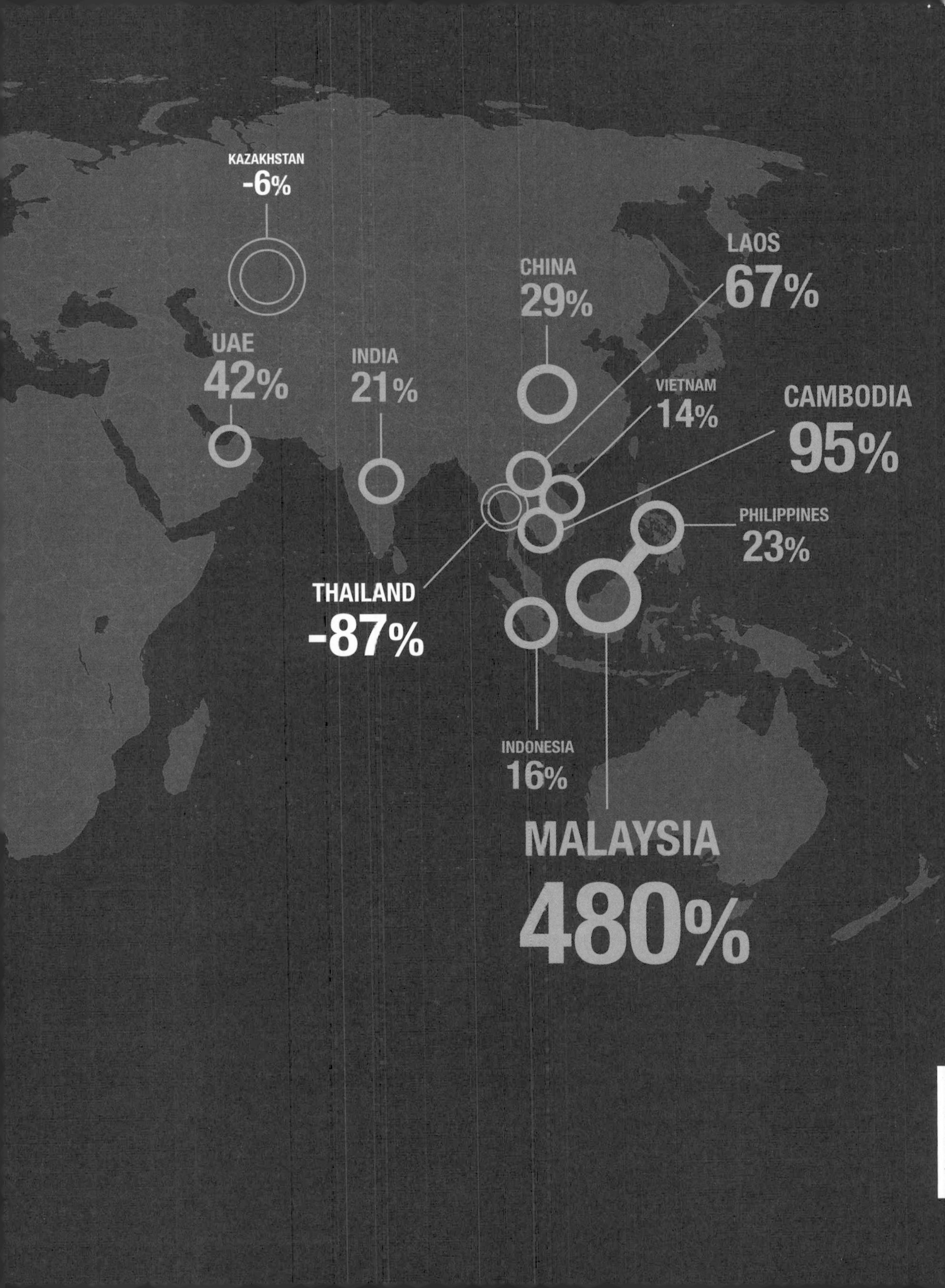

KAZAKHSTAN
-6%

CHINA
29%

LAOS
67%

UAE
42%

INDIA
21%

VIETNAM
14%

CAMBODIA
95%

PHILIPPINES
23%

THAILAND
-87%

INDONESIA
16%

MALAYSIA
480%

LEARNING FROM SINGAPORE

Singapore is a remarkable experiment in urban living. The epitome of melting pot of cultures, religions and traditions, Singapore is the place where Malay, Chinese, Indians and Westerners all live among one another. Consequently, Singapore has attracted the attention of social scientists from several disciplines and a wide range of ideological viewpoints. The island city state located at the tip of the Malay Peninsula is now home to some five million people, and has one of the highest per capita gross domestic products in the world. The impression the visitor receives is one of order, prosperity and modernity. Most of the population live in high-rise apartment blocks, and commute to their places of work on a public transport system which puts that of most western cities to shame. Car ownership is heavily taxed and those who do own cars tend to use them mainly for leisure activities, or for weekend trips to neighboring Malaysia; rush-hour traffic jams are unusual. The high-rise housing estates have little in common with their graffiti-daubed, run-down and violent counterparts in cities in Western Europe or the United States. They are clean, well-maintained, efficiently policed and mainly crime-free, and well-served by a variety of shops and hawker stalls, which provide mouth-watering Malay, Chinese, Indian, Phillipino, Korean, Indonesian and Japanese foods at very reasonable prices to locals and tourists alike.

Indeed, Singapore is not a static, monolithic region that is mutually exclusive from other cultures. Multiple identities, civilizations and value systems occupy the same space, as shown by the fact that Singapore is arguably the most ethnically, linguistically, religiously and environmentally dynamic regions in Asia. Singapore's heterogeneity does not undermine its regional identity. Nonetheless, a common history from the struggle against colonialism, coupled with growing economic interdependence, shared security concerns

MULTIPLE IDENTITIES, CIVILIZATIONS AND VALUE SYSTEMS OCCUPY THE SAME SPACE, AS SHOWN BY THE FACT THAT SINGAPORE IS ARGUABLY THE MOST ETHNICALLY, LINGUISTICALLY, RELIGIOUSLY AND ENVIRONMENTALLY DYNAMIC REGIONS IN ASIA.

and political cooperation fueled by the growth of a plethora of inclusive regional forums are helping to forge contemporary Singapore's urban identity.

Originally part of the Malaysian Federation consisting of Malaya Peninsula Sabah and Sarawak, Singapore was expelled from the federation in 1963 due to racial and economical tensions. Within decades, enforced by strong top down government policies, these two factors turn out to be Singapore's strongest draw in transforming this tiny city state into the richest and most livable country in South East Asia. Of the big influx of immigrants most came to Singapore with the agenda to achieve a higher standard of living and to get better opportunities which explains the large amount of Asian from poorer countries trying to "strike gold" in Singapore.

In the early days Singapore consisted of ethnically exclusive communities where Malay, Chinese and Indians can work together and roam the same public spaces but never live door to door. Through a resettlement program the government ensured an ethnic composition of every apartment block to be of "balanced" ethnic mix. Although an imposed planning strategy the resettlement program created the diverse Singapore we know today.

DIVERSITY BY DESIGN

Besides being a direct response to the housing shortages in the 1960's, The Housing and Development Act was the turning point towards the creation of the cultural mix in modern Singapore through intentional policy to group different races together within the same estate. Having achieved its stated goal of re-housing Singapore's squatters, many social problems were solved. By the early 1970's, about one-third of the population had been housed in HDB flats. HDB new towns were planned to be self-sufficient with commercial, recreational,institutional and other facilities to cater to the daily needs of the multi-ethnic population. In the 1980's, greater emphasis was placed on providing a quality living environment. The 'Precinct concept' was introduced to foster residents' cultural identity with their neighborhood and to promote social interaction. The precincts, comprising 400 to 600 dwelling units, were equipped with a landscaped open space for communal and recreational facilities. The aim is to create a 'Total Living Environment' to meet residents' needs for a quality living environment, recreation and accessibility to facilities. The 1990's saw increased emphasis on creating a quality and picturesque environment, as well as a strong visual identity for the precinct, neighborhood and town. Landmark buildings,

landscaping, open spaces, special architectural features and finishes helped to achieve a sense of identity and territorial exclusivity.

HIGH DENSITY LIVING

The Concept Plan of 2001, which set out the long-term strategic plan for Singapore, envisioned the creation of a livable city, providing a variety of housing locations and types. To plan for a scenario of a 5.5 million population and a reduction in household size, 800,000 new homes were needed, in addition to the 1 million dwelling units today. Given the constraints on the availability of land for new development, some of these new homes came from building more high density and very high-rise housing close to the city and Mass Rapid Transit stations in areas without restrictive height controls. Building additional homes in the city allowed more people to take advantage of the amenities that the city offers and live closer to where they work minimizing commutes.

The first super high-rise public housing estate is soon to be completed, and this is a watershed moment urban public housing policymaking: the future population is expected to stay in flats that are located at even greater heights. This new form of super high-rise, high density housing development opens up new challenges and calls for innovative methods in public housing management and maintenance. The social and environmental issues relating to high-rise, high-density living will also have to be addressed.

The physical design and planning of the public housing estates are considered important factors as they either obstruct or facilitate every-day social exchanges and community development. There are also concerns as to whether the kampong life (Malay term for village), characterized by its 'relaxed' pace of life, communitarian cooperation and happy days will be lost. Given the multi-racial and multi-religious make-up of Singapore's society, the town council plays an important role in facilitating and creating opportunities for residents to interact with one another in a more cohesive community. By encouraging greater public participation and community bonding, residents will be able to move up the Arnstein's ladder of citizen participation with increasing degrees of decision-making clout. In this way, residents should move away from tokenism and heavy reliance on the action of the public authority to solve their municipal problems.

MARRIAGE OF LAND AND ECONOMIC PLANNING

Singapore also has a land-use plan that is symbiotically connected to its economic growth. Districts are planned next to each other, overlaid within the green network of the Park Connector. Parks in Singapore has been merged into each district and serve as the linkage from one place to another. Parks for ordinary passive activities which require bigger space are provided adequately in the center and close to the center of the country; smaller parks suited for everyone's daily needs are attached into every sub-community. These parks reflect the usages in each district and become the transition space for the modern exchanging society. Besides the ordinary parks, other transition spaces are created in the city with different uses and different needs. Parks in the CBD area serve as the outdoor meeting place for lunch time, conferences, or office party time, while parks in the commercial district are for commercial exhibition, season at festival and occasional shows.

The Park Connector is the key which frames Singapore under the green city-planning concept. The green network works as linear linkages from one green piece to others. Parks in Singapore are highly dynamic in character to create a variety of public open space attractions for the residents and tourists.

The scale of the parks gradates from large scale in sub-urban area to small pocket parks in urban areas. Numbers of new parks are still increasing nowadays. Higher engineering technology allows parks to be created with fewer limitations. Sky Park is the new trend in the small land country. Tree top bridges and terraces attract all nature lovers to experience different parks.

PARKS IN SINGAPORE MERGE INTO EACH DISTRICT AND SERVE AS THE LINKAGE FROM ONE PLACE TO ANOTHER.

BEYOND INTEGRATION – A JOURNEY INTO THE HEART OF URBANISM

So what does all this for the future of urban housing trends in Singapore, Asia and beyond? What is the future for the multi cultural Singapore? Is enforced integration a good thing? Although very efficient it restricts the freedom of the people. Is there a better way to integrate people with different ethnical background than through housing strategies? In our ongoing journey to the heart of urbanism, Singapore's high density living with green space as the connections offers a sustainable solution from which other Asian cities might learn.

PROJECTIONS

BRANDING RISING TIGERS

BY CHRISTINA CRANE AND NING WONG, FUTUREBRAND

Fast economic growth can be a dizzying time for an emerging nation, and the instinct most developing economies have is to globalise and forget their past. Cultivating a city's sense of self and purpose keeps its government and residents true to the spirit of the city throughout the years of growing economy.

Fast-emerging Dubai has used its brand to establish its reputation as an international commercial centre with an innovative, dynamic and entrepreneurial business culture.[1] The brand idea of "excitement" describes and inspires its daring investments, awe-inspiring projects and encourages the competitive streak of its people. Its brand guides strong government policy and drives its citizenry to believe in the impossible goal.

While Dubai has chosen to look forward with its vision, most emerging market destinations find their brands defined by the tensions that exist between heritage and future, tradition and modern, local and global. Cities need to ensure these tensions impact the people, place and policy in a positive way, allowing a unique personality to develop.

With increasing competition, emerging cities are trying to attract investment with a combination of low-costs, capable talent and plentiful resources. The danger is that without differentiation, they compete more and more on a cost basis.

A CITY WITH A COMPELLING DIFFERENTIATOR – A BRAND – WILL HELP IT STAND OUT FROM COMPETITORS – FOR INVESTMENT, FOR TOURISM OR FOR RESIDENTS – TO CREATE SUSTAINABLE GROWTH AND REPUTATION.

DESTINATION BRANDING

A city or country brand isn't just a namesake or logo. A successful brand crystallises the unique DNA of a place, creating a compelling image and reputation in the mind of stakeholders – investors, residents or tourists.

A destination brand is built on four pillars: the physical place, the government's policies, the private sector and the people.

PLACE

Great historical cities were settled because of their geographic location – at the edge of a natural harbour, on the path of favourable sea tides, at the confluence of great rivers. Place can be one of the greatest strengths of a city, or one of the greatest barriers to overcome. When it comes to brand, place is the canvas for the future.

POLICY

The future of the city or country is shaped by government policy, through planning, targeting growth areas for investment and shaping the landscape through urban construction. Government policy drives the destination's vision, as well as creating the day to day controls that establish boundaries for its citizens and shape the urban or rural landscape. Policy enables interaction and ties the destination's heritage to its opportunities. It sets the brand's path for growth and establishes its competitive set.

PEOPLE

People drive the personality of the brand – the can-do spirit that epitomises Singapore, or the laid back style of Perth. Despite the many communities that make up a city or country, there is always a common thread that links them – a shared history has given the population a personality that can differentiate it from other destinations. Often, the people aren't aware of their shared values until they come under threat – with an influx of new residents or a change in government policy. This comes to life in the stories and rituals that weave into the fabric of daily life, as well as their actions in business and enterprise. The people create the narrative that makes a destination brand compelling.

GREAT DESTINATION BRANDS ARE FOUNDED IN HISTORY AND HERITAGE, AND CAN TAKE THE CITY INTO THE FUTURE THROUGH CENTRALISING THE GOVERNMENT'S VISION AROUND A CORE IDEA, AND BRINGING THE CULTURE OF THE CITY TO LIFE.

PRIVATE SECTOR

The private sector is the most visible expression of what a country or city values and can deliver. H&M and Ikea show Sweden's belief in accessible quality; Ducati and Gucci underline Italy's flair and style; BMW and Mercedes showcase Germany's precision, reliability and power.

Every city or country brand is a fusion of these four elements, building the reputation of the city, creating its stories and living its future. In the developed world, a brand can help the destination to communicate outwards, but in the case of cities in emerging countries, brand plays a stronger role internally: providing a rallying cry to bring the diverse citizenry together, which enables it to articulate a more cohesive vision of the city to the outside world.

BRAND SAIGON

Vietnam's largest city is a vibrant dance of culture and chaos. If emerging cities are defined by their balance of old and new, Ho Chi Minh City fits well into the mix.

Its move from royal kingdom to French colony, from war zone to communist nation is captured in the vibrant visual blend of French colonial architecture, warrens of cramped alleys filled with streetsellers, and modern office buildings. It is clear that Ho Chi Minh City is sprinting

towards the future – its economy has grown substantially in the 20 years since its economic liberalisation policies came into force, and it is benefitting from multinationals wanting to spread their risk and invest in an Asian economy outside of China. What is not clear is the government's vision for the future – aside from economic development, a differentiated path for growth is not immediately evident. There are dangers of the government and the people moving into the future with different objectives, and now is the time for the government to provide the citizens with an inspirational brand to evoke a rallying cry.

HO CHI MINH CITY AND ITS CITIZENS HAVE BEEN CONSTANT ADAPTORS THROUGHOUT THE CITY'S HISTORY.

The government and people already appear to be divided in some areas, the most obvious being the name of the city: Ho Chi Minh City is the name used by the populace only when dealing with government. Saigon, the popular name of the city since the 17th century, is still used in everyday language and print even thought it is the official name for one neighbourhood only. The dichotomy is deepened by the personality of each – serious Ho Chi Minh City and lively Saigon. If the city does not begin to communicate a vision to gel the people together, the risk is that it becomes like any other emerging market city in 10 years.

If a destination brand is built from four pillars – people, place, private sector and policy, Ho Chi Minh City is an interesting case. The place clearly defines the chaotic way people move and interact, the people are resilient, ingenious and adaptable, the private sector is entrepreneurial and proud and the government is staid. There is a tension between the first three and the government, and while the government tries to develop the economy in an equitable way, the people do not trust them because of the high level of corruption. The government needs to harness the momentum, rather than working against it, to deliver a cohesive vision.

When looking at these four elements, Saigon is strongly led by its people, and their pride can give the city a personality that cannot be matched by other emerging competitors. It is for this reason that the brand is Saigon, not Ho Chi Minh City.

SAIGON RETAINS THE CULTURE, THE RITUALS AND THE STORIES OF THE PAST – WHICH CAN BE LEVERAGED TO CREATE A BRAND THAT ENABLES STRONG GROWTH WHILE MAINTAINING ITS COMMUNITY SPIRIT.

People: adaptable, resilient, charismatic, resourceful, inventive, celebratory, proud.

Place: colonial charm versus mad motorcycles; chaotic creativity; post-war historical landmarks; rendezvous city where all come together.

Private: entrepreneurial, adaptable, localising global concepts.

Policy: capitalism versus communism; equitable growth; directive.

The brand: Enabling ingenuity, embracing chances.

Saigon could build its brand around the entrepreneurial spirit of the people, which can allow it to build competencies in innovation and design in the future. Concurrently, it ensures the retention of the rustic, humble nature of Saigon that would encourage overseas Saigonese to come home to roost, to educate and inspire its local residents with a world of possibilities.

In order to bring the brand to life, the government could look at harnessing existing strengths in its people and private sector through initiatives such as investing in art schools to build a generation of lateral thinkers, connecting entrepreneurs through urban business communities or making it easier for people to take chances through offering startup loans or grants for SMEs.

If Saigon wants to differentiate itself in the future, it needs to begin to set itself on a new path now – more than economic development, the city's vision should leverage the best of the people and of the place. Saigon is chaos, but within chaos lies a creative soul. This could set it apart from the rest of Asia.

IF THE GOVERNMENT SHOWS SUPPORT FOR THE INGENUITY OF ITS PEOPLE, IT CAN BUILD AN ENTREPRENEURIAL BRAND – A COMPELLING STORY FOR ANY MULTINATIONAL SEEKING TO INVEST IN A NEW LOCATION.

4 CITIES – 4 IDE

A PHOTOGRAPHIC ESSAY OF COMPARISON

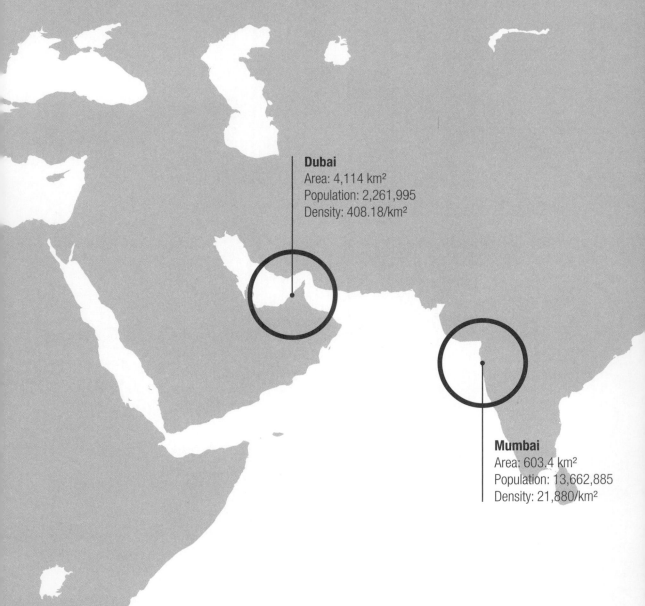

Dubai
Area: 4,114 km²
Population: 2,261,995
Density: 408.18/km²

Mumbai
Area: 603.4 km²
Population: 13,662,885
Density: 21,880/km²

TITIES

Bangkok
Area: 1,568.737 km²
Population: 8,160,522
Density: 4,051/km²

Manila
Area: 38.55 km²
Population: 1,660,714
Density: 43,079/km²

BANGKOK

DUBAI

MANILA

MUMBAI

485

MANILA

MUMBAI

BANGKOK

DUBAI

MANILA

MUMBAI

BANGKOK

DUBAI

MANILA

MUMBAI

BANGKOK

DUBAI

MANILA

MUMBAI

BANGKOK

DUBAI

MANILA

MUMBAI

BANGKOK

DUBAI

MANILA

MUMBAI

BANGKOK

MUMBAI

MANILA

DUBAI

BANGKOK

DUBAI

MANILA

MUMBAI

สีลม
Si Lom

2 ♿↕

MRTA

M
MRT

BANGKOK

محطة
بر دبي
Bur Dubai
Station

Dubaiabra
دبي عبرة

Dubaiwaterbus
دبي ووتر باص

DUBAI

MANILA

MUMBAI

BANGKOK

DUBAI

MANILA

MUMBAI

BANGKOK

DUBAI

MUMBAI

MANILA

BANGKOK

DUBAI

MANILA

MUMBAI

BANGKOK

DUBAI

MANILA

MUMBAI

MANILA

MUMBAI

BANGKOK

DUBAI

MANILA

MUMBAI

ONE WAY
CITY OF MANILA

BENAVIDEZ ST.
BRGY. 260 ZONE 24
DISTRICT II

DONATED BY:
JADEWELL PARKING

HAPPY WEDE
902 Benavidez Street, Binondo

MANILA

बृहन्मुंबई महानगरपालिका
सी - विभाग
विना पेरीवाला विभाग

MUMBAI

MANILA

MITSUBISHI DIGITAL

MUMBAI

BANGKOK

DUBAI

MANILA

MUMBAI

URBAN FUTURE

CLOSING

Today's Asia is a vast, energetic slice of the Earth. Ever emergent, it is a place that challenges our profession. It is billions of people, on the go, upwardly mobile. It is aggressive in its encroachment on natural habitats. The projections of energy consumption are mind-boggling. 17 of the world's 25 largest groupings of people are here. These places are joined by more than 160 others cities with more than a million people. The statistics and images of the revolution underway can be overpowering, painting a picture of growth run amok.

The adjectives are consistent: Multi-faceted, colorful, and frenetic; and scale – both as an ordering principle and as a method of measurement – has an omnipresence that is almost brutal. Against the numbers posed by ChIndia, even America's size seems infantile. This all brings to mind the inevitable questions. What will we do when 3.7 billion people all drive to work? What will we do when these same people all want air conditioned McMansions? What will we do when they all can travel the globe, passports eagerly in hand? The answer to these questions is emphatically, "look around."

People want these things now. Precedent shows that after hunger and strife, comes the automobile and air conditioning. It is the natural order of things. The questions we are asking shouldn't be about what we do when they want, but what do we do when they can? It is this paradigm shift, currently underway, which will have the greatest impact on the character of built, natural and social environments.

But does this impact necessarily have to be negative? The conventional wisdom is yes. Our different media are full of doomsday scenarios. There are the nightmares of millions of Chinese and Indians each armed with a Hummer, a track home and a frequent flyer card. There are the frightening visions of multiple ski resorts in the midst of inhospitable Arabian deserts. This is all plausible, but we are beginning to perceive something different at play in Asia's transformation.

One encouraging sign is the intensification of Asia's urbanization. The region's growth is mostly urban in nature, and it is this that will be its saving grace. There is sprawl, but it could be a lot worse. In many places in Asia, contemporary middle classes are satisfied with small apartments, are accustomed to public transport and sharing open spaces. Hong Kong, Singapore and Seoul are good examples of wealthy Asian cities – places that have reached high levels of development but have done so in a relatively sustainable way. Barring some exceptions in Singapore, this has largely been an accidental process.

The GDP per capita of the average Hongkonger is just over $37,000 per year; for an American, S44,000 per year. Not much difference. But the average American emits 20.4 tons of carbon dioxide per year, while the typical Hongkonger manages to get through only 5.36. Is it a coincidence that America's population density is tiny compared to Hong Kong's more than 16,000 per square kilometer, just as a resident of Hong Kong has a carbon footprint only a quarter of the size of an American's? Is it a coincidence that nearly nine out of ten Americans own a car, while only one of five of those in Hong Kong do? No, they are not coincidences. They are circumstances, ones that need not be forgotten elsewhere on the continent.

Today's Asia may seem like an endless and overwhelming forest of cities, much in the same spirit as Koolhaas' adage that "the city is an addictive machine from which there is no escape." But, this is good. It is only within the context of cities that the remarkable challenges posed by Asia's projected growth can be mitigated. By relentlessly urbanizing just as it gets into the groove of its own economic development, Asia can use the template of the city to tame the adverse impacts of its growth. As hundreds of millions of people move into cities, and dozens of new cities are being built in what is amounting to history's biggest building spree, we must remind ourselves that the city can be an aggressively green instrument. That is why in Asia, it is critical that we build the smart cities of the future, and we build them now.

IN ASIA, IT IS CRITICAL THAT WE BUILD THE SMART CITIES OF THE FUTURE, AND WE BUILD THEM NOW.

These are cities with efficient and extensive public transport and ample public space. These cities will need to be buttressed by a culture of expectations and education, one where citizens are fulfilled by a reduced footprint, a smaller place to call home, a walk to work, an appreciation for the delicate balance between man and nature. There are glimmers of this already. The combination of scale and the moral urgency brought on by overactive development can transform the Asian story into one that heralds the most innovative urban design, where planning can take on a renewed green savvy. For the rest of the world, let us hope that there may be positive lessons that we will learn from here. The construction cranes from Shanghai to Mumbai to Dubai speak not just of hyper-growth, but of abundant possibility.

SOURCES

52-61 Central Statistics Office Afghanistan, Bangladesh Bureau of Statistics, National Institute of Statistics of Cambodia, Data Center for Resources and Environmental Sciences of the Chinese Academy of Sciences, Census and Statistics Department of the Hong Kong Special Administrative Region, Indonesia Statistics Yearbook, Office of the Registrar General and Census Commissioner of India, Statistics Center of Iran, Iraq Ministries of Trade and Planning, Central Bureau of Statistics of the State of Israel, Statistics Bureau Japan, Department of Statistics Jordan, Ministry of Planning of the State of Kuwait, Central Administration of Statistics for the Republic of Lebanon, Nepal Central Bureau of Statistics, Pakistan Population Census Organization, National Statistics Office of the Philippines, Central Department of Statistics of the Kingdom of Saudi Arabia, Singapore Department of Statistics, Department of Census and Statistics of Sri Lanka, Central Bureau of Statistics of the Syrian Arab Republic, Ministry of the Interior of the Republic of China (Taiwan), Ministry of the Economy of the United Arab Emirates, General Statistics Office of Vietnam, Britannica Book of the Year 2006 and 2007, UN World Urbanization Prospects 2005 Report, the 2007 CIA Factbook and the 2004 United Nations Demographic Yearbook.

62-63 City Mayors (Institute), "The World's Fastest Growing Cities and Urban Areas from 2006 to 2020."

66-67 United Nations Statistics Division, Series name and code: Carbon dioxide emissions (CO_2), thousand metric tons of CO_2 (CDIAC/MDG) [code 30249]

68-69 United Nations Statistics Division, Series name and code: Carbon dioxide emissions (CO_2), metric tons of CO_2 per capita (CDIAC/MDG) [code 30248]. Last updated 4 Oct 2007.

70-71 China Central Television.

72-73 United Nations Statistics Division, Series name and code: Carbon dioxide emissions (CO_2), metric tons of CO_2 per capita (CDIAC/MDG) [code 30248]. Last updated 4 Oct 2007.

74-75 World Bank China Data and Statistics Database. World Health Organization Global InfoBase.

94-95 United Nations Statistics Division, Series name and code: Water, percentage of population with access to improved drinking water sources, total, urban and rural/MDG [code 27910]. Last updated 8 October 2007.

98-99 United Nations Statistics Division, Series name and code: Water, percentage of population with access to improved drinking water sources, total, urban and rural/MDG [code 27910]. Last updated 8 October 2007.

100-103 United Nations Statistics Division, Series Name: Sanitation, percentage of population with access to improved sanitation, total, urban and rural/MDG [185 countries, 1990-2004].

112-113 United Nations Statistics Division, Series name and code: Protected area to total surface area, percentage (UNSD calculated from UNEP-WCMC/MDG) [code 29981]. The World Conservation Union, 2007 International Union for the Conservation of Nature (IUCN) Red List of Threatened Animals.

116-117 The World Conservation Union, 2007
International Union for the Conservation
of Nature (IUCN) Red List of Threatened Animals.

118-119 United Nations Statistics Division, Series name
and code: Protected area to total surface area,
percentage (UNSD calculated from UNEP-
WCMC/MDG) [code 29981].

120-121 United Nations Statistics Division, based
on estimates gathered by the Food and
Agricultural Organization (FAO) of the United
Nations.Series name and code: Forested
land area as percentage of land area (FAO
estimates/MDG) [code 3740].

138-139 Shanghai Municipal Government, Xinhua
News Agency, *Jiefang Daily.*

140-141 *World Gazetteer,* and the United Nations
Department of Economic and Social Affairs.

142-143 *World Gazetteer,* National Media Council
of the UAE.

154-155 Emporis.com.

156-157 Emporis.com.

164-165 National Media Council of the UAE.

166-167 China People's Educational Press. International
Center for Chinese Language and Culture.

168-169 Mumbai Metropolitan Region Development
Authority (MMRDA).

170-173 Calculation made via Google Earth.

188-189 Calculation made via Emporis.

196-197 *China Daily.*

254-257 Shanghai Municipal Government and
the World Bank.

258-259 The World Bank.

260-261 2007 United Arab Emirates Yearbook,
Dubai Municipality, National Media Council
of the United Arab Emirates.

262-263 Skytrax World Airport Awards.

264-265 Airport Authority Hong Kong;
Beijing International Capital Airport Co., Ltd;
Qatar Civil Aviation Authority;
Civil Aviation Authority of Dubai.

276-277 Office for Metropolitan Architecture,
Zaha Hadid Architects, Foster and Partners,
Paul Andreu Architects.

290-291 Macau SAR Government Statistics
and Census Service.

306-307 United Nations Education, Social and Cultural
Organization (UNESCO).

308-309 *Travel and Leisure* 'World's Best' Awards.

310-311 Asiahotels.com, Department of Tourism
& Commerce of Dubai, Vietnam National
Administration of Tourism.

314-317 *Forbes* magazine.

318-319 United Nations Conference and Trade and Development.

320-321 World Health Organization Global Database on Body Mass Index.

322-323 *Forbes* magazine.

324-325 Louis Vuitton.

326-327 Carrefour, Tesco and WalMart.

338-339 Skytrax World Airport Awards.

340-341 Calculated by researching Air China, Cathay Pacific and Emirates route maps/ destination lists.

354-355 Calculated from data available in the *CIA World Factbook*

372-373 India Tour Operators Promotion Council, Shanghai Municipal Statistics Bureau, National Media Council of the UAE.

374-375 TV5 Monde, British Broadcasting Corporation, China Central Television, Costa Coffee, Starbucks.

376-377 *China Daily* and the Rajiv Gandhi National Institute of Youth Development.

378-381 United Nations Economic and Social Commission for Asia and the Pacific.

384-385 United Nations Economic and Social Commission for Asia and the Pacific.

416-417 UNHabitat (United Nations Human Settlement Program) Slum Estimates Database.

426-427 http://www.brandchannel.com/features_profile. asp?pr_id=238

CONTRIBUTORS

EDITORS	Sean Chiao
	Daniel Elsea
	Oanh Thi Nguyen
ESSAYS	Jody Brown
	Denise Scott Brown
	Christopher Choa
	Cobe Architects
	Christina Crane
	Daniel Elsea
	Stephen Engblom
	Cheng Sze Hon
	David Jung
	Naonori Matsuda
	Kerry McWalter
	Eve Sanguanruang
	Philip Schmunk
	Ning Wong
	Yiwen Zhu
INFOGRAPHICS	Morn Associates Designers
PHOTOGRAPHY	Vorrarit Anantsorrarak
	Dixi Carrillo
	Robin Kuang
	David Lloyd
	Sirintira Maneesri
	Torlarp Nimsrisukkul
	Dino Paxenos
RESEACHERS	Hugo Errazuriz
	Feng He
	Eva Huang
	Antonio Lao
	Changxia (Eva) Li
	Leon Li
	Kimberlee Myers
	Madeleine Sembring
	Huang Yan
	Jason Yeh
	Melody Yiu
	YunFei Zhao
	Jutta Kehrer

PHOTO CREDITS

DAVID LLOYD — Cover, 1, 8-13, 30-47, 72-73, 96-97, 102-103, 114-115, 128-130, 138-143, 146-151, 164-165, 178-179, 181, 186-187, 204-205, 208-211, 214-217, 231-234, 241 *bottom*, 248-251, 282-287, 302-303, 305, 309, 336-337, 352 *left*, 353 *right*, 358-361, 382-383, 394-395, 398-401, 403-407, 409-413, 436-440, 441 *bottom*, 442-445, 446 *bottom*, 447-450, 451 *bottom*, 452-467, 469 *top*, 470-473, 476-477, 484

DINO PAXENOS — 14-21, 252-253, 304, 352 *right*, 390-391, 441 *top*, 451 *top*, 468 *top*, 469 *bottom*

DIXI CARRILLO — 26-29, 50-51, 64-65, 70-71, 74-75, 104-105, 108-109, 111, 180, 182-184, 188-197, 200-203, 206-207, 212-213, 218-219, 221-223, 225-227, 229, 236-240, 241 *top*, 242-245, 262-263, 268-271, 274-275, 280-281, 292-293, 296-297, 300-301, 308, 322-323, 338-339, 363, 366-369, 388-389, 392-393, 396-397, 402

ALFRED MOLON — 80-81

ALEX DE DIOS — 312-313, 376-377

ROBIN KUANG — 331

VORRARIT ANANTSORRARAK — 346-347, 349

©iStockphoto.com/SimonGurney — 420-421

©iStockphoto.com/syagci — 428-429

©iStockphoto.com/laughingmango — 433